VOLUME 5

BUSINESS LEADERS EDITION

MISSION MATTERS

World's Leading Entrepreneurs Reveal their
TOP TIPS TO SUCCESS

ADAM TORRES AND ROMAN TSAROVSKY

Century City, CA

Listen to our
PODCASTS

MISSION MATTERS
WE AMPLIFY STORIES

www.MissionMatters.com

DEDICATION

This is dedicated to all those who are working diligently each
and every day to help the world work together.

TABLE OF CONTENTS

ACKNOWLEDGMENTS

I would like to thank my family for their ongoing love and support. Every moment I spend working is a moment away from them but at the end of the day, everything I do is for them. I would like to express my gratitude and appreciation for my team at Ally, without whom none of this would be possible. I am grateful for our clients who took a leap of faith with a small startup software company that set out to solve some fundamental problems caused by third-party marketplaces. I'm happy we have helped so many businesses keep their revenue and their customers by cutting out unnecessary middlemen. I'm also thankful to the drivers who are out there every day working to get people their food, medicine, groceries, and anything else they could possibly need. Those same drivers are now able to keep everything they earn. As always, I can't express enough my appreciation for my loving family, my friends, and everyone I work with to bring our vision to the world.

FOREWORD

By **ADAM TORRES**

If there were a zodiac symbol for the "year of the pivot," it definitely would have applied to 2020. From Fortune 500 companies to mom and pop shops in our local communities, hundreds of businesses pivoted to add value to the marketplace. Entrepreneurs found themselves using ingenuity and resources to provide much-needed services, save businesses and lives, and maintain cashflow during the pandemic.

On our daily Mission Matters podcasts and YouTube channels we featured hundreds of businesses in 2020 that pivoted, sometimes overnight, to lend their expertise during quarantine. For example, one manufacturing shop in Chicago went from producing displays for tradeshows to making hundreds of thousands of face shields for our front line workers. Another company went from importing merch for concerts headlined by some of the top names in music to executing deals on large orders of face masks and hand sanitizer.

One of the things that surprised me most during this year of interviews were how many entrepreneurs were working on projects that coincidentally became essential during the pandemic. One company I spoke with was producing a highly secure video communications platform designed to help executives discuss sensitive information. This solution became a staple at many companies due to the pandemic, accelerating the company's growth far beyond what they'd planned for.

Another outcome of the pandemic that was surprising to me was the amount of innovation that took place. For example, the health-care sector went through a renaissance. With the wider acceptance of telemedicine, suddenly anyone could connect with a doctor or other medical professional almost immediately. Doctors, patients, healthcare systems, insurance carriers and technology providers all came together to accelerate the delivery of services in a time span that would not have been considered prior to a worldwide event such as the pandemic. With this new level of care and choice being set, it is likely that the work that was started will continue on a path of improvement.

Though not experienced firsthand on our shows, a likely outcome of the pandemic is that a new generation of entrepreneurs will be inspired due to their experiences in quarantine. Kids that found themselves with schools shut down, suddenly confined to "pods" with select classmates and their parents at home, are already shaping what our world will look like in the next 20 years in their minds. Really exciting to consider what the next generation is dreaming up.

I should note that we did have one child on one of our shows in 2020 who sold hand painted rocks on Facebook. This kid is as smart and industrious as they come. Such an inspiration. His sales went way up due to more people spending time on Facebook. Alternatively, my good friends' son experienced first hand what can happen when your revenue shrinks to zero due to a shutdown. His "bubblegum machine empire" dream had to be re-evaluated when his machines no longer received traffic since the restaurant locations where his machines earned were shut down. He was in the process of scaling when the pandemic hit and had just acquired a few new machines.

What a lesson to learn during such a young age. Business is sometimes not fair and even a good well-thought-out plan can fail. These two young entrepreneurs give me hope for our future.

Above I shared many of the successes that have come about due to the pandemic. But we of course cannot forget the fact that many businesses lost revenue or failed entirely, nor that so many lives were lost. But I'd like to leave you with a little story that an entrepreneur told me during the pandemic that I draw on for hope and inspiration frequently. It's the story of the little ox.

When the little ox is young he will dream big and be bold. The little ox is fearless and does not think about the possibility of failure. If the little ox wants to go to the moon or to Mars, he will make plans and bet everything on this possibility.

But with each failure or defeat along the way, the little ox grows a little older and a little more cautious. Until one day, the little ox is wearing a yoke plowing the fields, doing what all the other big oxen are doing. He has given up on his grand ideas and dreams.

Every time I face a defeat, I try to channel the "little ox" within to force me to be brave and to continue moving forward, rather than settling for becoming more like the "big ox" who puts up with a life without dreams.

As you read this book, it is my hope that you will gain inspiration and ideas from the many authors who continue to inspire and innovate by sharing their stories of both triumph and at times, defeat.

If we collectively channel our "little ox" within, we will continue to move forward in our families, communities, nation and world.

To your success,

Adam Torres

P.S. If you'd like to apply to be a guest on one of our shows visit **MissionMatters.com/PodcastGuest** to apply.

INTRODUCTION

By **ROMAN TSAROVSKY**

Building a sustainable business that you love and are proud of doesn't have to take years of trial and error. It's built on four fundamental principles that can't be ignored if you want a successful business.

It's really simple actually and it's what you will soon figure out for yourself throughout the pages of this book.

For far too long so many courageous entrepreneurs go through years and years of trial and error. And as statistics show, many businesses close within the first 5 years of operation. Barely turning a profit.

What I'm here to do is help you avoid those pitfalls and make sure you know exactly what goes into creating a business that thrives and helps others get what they want out of life.

But before we get to that, let's discuss a few important things in order for you to really attain the goals and dreams that you have.

For starters, a common misbelief is that you need to know exactly what you want to do when you start out in business. Like you have to have this unforeseen prophecy in your mind that says "I'm going to do this and I'm going to be super successful". However, that is the first thing I want to talk about.

You don't need to have it all figured out right away.

Let me give you a bit of context about where I started and how it all came together for me. And then we'll move into the four main major areas of ANY business in order for you to be successful and profitable over an extended period of time.

Allowing you to scale your business and have it running in a way that gives you more time, more control over your decision-making for yourself as well as for your clients, and their customers depending on what business you start.

Sound good?

Let's hop in the time machine and head back to where it all began for me.

Looking back, I'd like to say being an entrepreneur was in my DNA and I always knew I would run a multi-million dollar business.

But that is far from the truth.

As a teenager, I really didn't know what I wanted out of life. And growing up with a lot less than most didn't help me come to any epiphanies any faster. There was no road map for me or blueprint in the beginning that led me towards what kind of business I should begin with.
Or how to even start.

And you might be surprised to know that's where many successful entrepreneurs start out.

Confused and pondering the ever-pressing question "where should I even start?".

For me, my journey started with tragedy. Losing my mother at an early age really opened my eyes to taking responsibility for my life. It was a huge wake-up call for me.

I learned nothing is permanent.

Since I was very young I didn't know what I wanted to do. I only knew that I had a work ethic to do things far more thoroughly than most. I started paying attention to the opportunities that were around me and started working as an assistant financial advisor.

As a youth, I hated work which is normal. But I learned a lot of good things. I focused on the work and just did it. I took my series seven, became a financial advisor, and started consulting. I started helping people and working with big brand names and individuals but I didn't have any job satisfaction.

This was the first sign and nudge towards realizing I needed to do something different. I remember it very clearly—the moment it all changed for me.

It was 2008, and the financial industry was really falling apart. But did well for my clients. My execution was stellar and I improved one client's performance above-market performance by 18%. But here's the turn.

The representative from that company saw the results but showed no real value of appreciation or anything. He basically said, good job, thank you, and bye.

Not in the sense I wasn't good but, more like this was no big deal.

That was the moment I made a change and the key point here. I saw that was a problem, realized there was something I could do about it, and started my very own consulting firm shortly after.

But I also did something many people fail to do.

I did not damage the relationships I made. I instead leveraged the connections. But as a new entrepreneur, I made many mistakes.

I didn't manage expectations, I didn't return calls, and didn't focus on improving better relationships over time. I had some success but became tired and burned out because I rarely said no to work in the beginning.

I had to make another change and ask some tough questions.

Which ultimately led me to the mechanism I use today—finding the fundamental truths of how all successful businesses work. I generally understood the similarities between all businesses and realized that it's all about four things.

I refocused and started from scratch, running my consulting firm for the past 13 years with this idea. And it's been very successful. Allowing me to still maintain a wonderful relationship with the very first client I started with.

I focused on consulting, building businesses, developing and automating parts of the business, and using machine learning to deliver on my promises. Although things improved I found myself repeating the same structure over and over again and knew there was a better way.

So I worked towards no longer focusing on consulting. But instead, began creating solutions that will fundamentally change and provide tools for people to change how they operate, how they do their business, and creating the whole platform of having other choices.

I set out to solve larger problems with technology. And in the beginning, it was hard. Once again, I had to give up good money– Back to something that was a question mark.

It was the best decision I could have made. And now harness the fundamental understanding of business, a fundamental understanding of relationships, and two core principles you will learn that took me years to figure out.

To circle back. There are many reasons you may want to start a business. It can begin with wanting more freedom, or simply providing a better life for your family.

Whatever the reason, learning these core pillars to starting and maintaining a business that stands the test of time is essential. Lucky for you by the end of this book you won't ever question how it's done.

Welcome to *Mission Matters: Business Leaders, Vol. 5.* In this book, you're going to learn how to make leaps and bounds in your approach to managing business and people. You're going to remove all confusion in all of your processes, build better relationships, give yourself more time and infuse purpose in what you're doing every day.

My experience towards building a better business, taught me nothing is permanent, things are always evolving. And business is no different. It is my deepest wish that core concepts of business leadership offer you as much success and happiness as it has given me.

To your unlimited success,

Roman Tsarovsky

CHAPTER 1

THE TRUE COST OF BAD SERVICE

By **CHRISTINE CHURCHILL BURKE**

Most business leaders think investing in customer service is a waste of money.

There is a common misconception that if money is spent to train the customer service team, or invest in customer-facing technology or process improvement initiatives, that these investments are simply a cost to the company that result in minimal benefits. They may make things easier for the customer service team, but they don't actually pay for themselves, let alone make money for the company.

But that assumption is just not accurate. In fact, the opposite is true. Investing in customer service is one of the best moves a company can make to increase revenue, slash costs, and grow profits.

Let's start with some statistics from recent studies on customer service.

- 67% of customer churn is preventable if companies resolve issues the first time they occur (Ameyo)
- One-third of consumers say they would consider switching companies after just one instance of bad customer service (American Express)

- 91% of customers who are unhappy with a brand will just leave without complaining or saying anything about it (Kolsky)
- Increasing customer retention rates by only 5% increases profits by 25% to 95% (Harvard Business School)

What do these stats tell us?

Two things.

1. Having really good customer service both saves and makes companies a lot of money. (Replacing lost customers with new ones is WAY more expensive than continuing to serve existing ones.)

2. Having bad customer service hurts companies in ways they may not be aware of. (Customers who leave after the first problem, without telling you they're leaving, don't give you a lot of data on what you're doing wrong--or even THAT you're doing anything wrong.)

This is why there's such a big disconnect around investing in customer service. Most companies think the path to great ROI is in sales, because sales brings in new customers and contracts. And that's often true...in the short term. But they overlook how much of ROI is directly tied to customer service, and the overall customer experience, in the long term.

To say that this issue derives from a lack of leadership knowledge and understanding of their overall customer experience is an understatement. Studies these days are showing that executives of manufacturing and service companies, for instance, tend to think the cost of bad service (COBS) is about 5% of their companies' gross sales...but the *actual* COBS often ranges as high as 30%. Whether this ignorance is willful or accidental, that's a staggering difference for the people in charge to not be aware of.

Specifically, there are two types of costs associated with bad service. I like to call them the visible cost and the invisible cost.

The visible cost of bad service is what I mentioned earlier: how much it costs to get new customers instead of (or at least in addition to) continuing to serve your existing ones. It also includes all the time and money spent on fixing mistakes, correcting problems, dealing with complaints, and doing work over again that's already been done at least once. Plus all the money spent on refunds, legal fees, commission payments on canceled sales, and so on.

Most business leaders are aware of visible costs at least up to a point, but they tend to treat them as normal, unavoidable, or just the costs of doing business...which blinds them to the possibility of improving them and reinforces the misconception that investing in customer service is just throwing good money after bad.

Visible costs add up fast, and you might think they're the bigger of the two costs. But invisible costs often account for even larger losses to an organization.

Think about it: how much money could your ideal customer bring in? Now that you have that number in your head, imagine that ideal customer's best friend or former boss or professional mentor or next-door neighbor, a former customer of yours, telling them in excruciating detail how terrible your customer service is. So the ideal customer doesn't even get in touch with you—which means you lost that amazing amount of money *and you never even knew.*

That's what makes these costs invisible—things like bad word-of-mouth and a low reputation for customer service are things you may never be aware of. And because you're not aware of them, you'll never look to fix them, which perpetuates the bad customer service that makes the invisible costs worse...it's a vicious circle.

So the real question here isn't "can you afford to invest in customer service?", it's "can you afford *not* to?"

The good news is, there are several straightforward steps any business leader can take to not only justify investing in customer service improvement, but also start to turn the costs of bad service into benefits of better service.

The first step is simply to understand the problem—and to admit that it *is* a problem. The first part of this chapter should have helped you to start doing that. But knowing, as they say, is only half the battle. What else can you do to fix problematic customer service and make sure your investment in it is effective?

Here are four steps I've found to be successful in almost every type and size of business.

Understand Your Specific Costs

You've heard the adage "what gets measured, gets managed." As you've now seen, the real costs of bad customer service are rarely measured--likely because no one ever actually plans on having to do work over or make mistakes that then have to be fixed. When issues like that come up, it's easy (and more comfortable) to treat them as anomalies or flukes rather than actual costs to plan for.

When you start putting an actual dollar amount on the results of bad service, you'll start to see the value in improving it. Some good questions to ask here include:

- How much do you pay your customer service employees?
- How long does it typically take one of them to fix a mistake, check on a problematic order, or redo work for a customer?
- How frequently do customers need to call back about an issue that was never followed up on or a previous issue that was not resolved thoroughly?
- How often do these employees need to resolve customer-facing issues that should have never occurred?
- How typical is it that customer issues get escalated?

Put those numbers together and you'll start to see the annual visible cost of customer service issues.

I once worked with a logistics company in Australia that got a lot of complaints from clients that their waybills (basically the shipping labels) weren't accurate. The company's drivers were supposed to check these waybills before accepting and loading pickups but they weren't doing it consistently. When asked, most of the drivers didn't think that requirement was all that important or necessary, even though it was part of their job description. Even the leaders of the company weren't all that concerned. After all, it was only a few seconds of looking at a piece of paper–how much difference could it really make?

The company got a shock when I actually ran the numbers. It turns out that if the drivers simply spending an extra five to seven seconds confirming the accuracy of the waybill before loading the shipment would save the company almost 2 million dollars a year in reworking costs. When the company president heard that, he immediately ordered his training staff to work with the drivers to make sure they understood the importance of accurate waybills!

And this example only showcased the visible cost associated with this process glitch, NOT the invisible costs. Remember, part of invisible costs will also be the drain on employee engagement when they are distracted from their tasks in order to fix an issue that should not have occurred in the first place.

You can ask similar questions with invisible costs like I did above: How much does a typical customer bring in? How much does it cost to find a new one vs. nurture an existing one? How many customers do we lose because of customer service issues we do not know about? How many referrals does a typically happy customer bring us? Those questions together can tell you how many customers you may be losing or turning away without knowing about it.

Understand Your Customer's Actual Experience

If you run a company, you probably think you know exactly what your customer's experience is like. You know your product, your marketing, your infrastructure, and your people, so you know what your customers will go through, right?

Not likely.

In this case, knowing everything so well actually works against you. Most of us are way too close to our own organizations to know what our customers actually experience. We know what we *think* it is (or at least what we hope it is!), but we rarely know how it *actually* is.

The solution? Mystery shop your own company. Take a day or two and become a customer. Order a product, then try to return it. Call your own customer service number and see how long you sit on hold. Pretend you've never visited your website, then go there and try to find something without any help. Schedule a service call anonymously and see if the provider shows up on time.

Trust me, this will be an eye-opener. You'll find issues and inefficiencies you had no idea were even possible. Some of them may be flukes or one-off issues, but a lot of them won't be.

For example, this exercise helped the leaders of a prominent insurance company understand that their customers had to go through an unconscionable amount of effort to close accounts after the death of a loved one. Bereaved family members would have to make multiple calls across multiple lines, explain their story to several different departments, provide many copies of death certificates, etc...adding all kinds of stress to some of the most vulnerable and tragic moments of their lives. Realizing this, the company instituted a centralized team protocol with one and only one point of contact for each bereaved family.

Which brings me to the next step…

Determine Your Customer's Pain Points

Mystery shopping your company will give you a good start on knowing what your customers struggle with. Here are two other ways to supplement that one with:

1.   Ask them!

Not every customer will answer a survey, especially if it's tacked onto a long customer service call. But customers do tend to respond well when a company makes an honest effort to learn what would make their experience better. If you reach out to them sincerely and ask them for feedback, many will take you up on it. (And clearly you'll get at least SOME complaints anyway, so look for patterns in them to show where common issues crop up.) Be open and let your customers know WHY their feedback is important and valued.

2.   Ask your employees!

I'm going to let you in on a trade secret here: the #1 thing you pay consultants for is to tell you things your employees would tell you (and likely are already telling you) for free—or at least, for no more than you're already paying them.

If there's one group of people who will gladly tell you when something isn't working, it's your employees. They want you to know so you can fix it! And there's nothing more frustrating for them than to tell you about an issue, only to have you ignore them until a high-paid consultant tells you about the same thing months or years later.

Customer-facing employees will know a lot of customer pain points because they see and hear about those pain points constantly. So ask those employees what those pain points are, and take their word as gospel.

Doing this guided a large telecommunications company to realize that while each of their departments were doing their jobs well, the messaging and customer support across departments was wildly inconsistent, resulting in a confusing and subpar customer experience. By realigning their messaging and support protocols across the whole company, the organization leaders not only created a more seamless customer experience and resolved multiple pain points, but also increased employee engagement by showing the staff how valuable their feedback was.

And speaking of employees…

Invest In Your Employee Experience

Your customer experience will 100% reflect your employee experience. Happy employees give good customer service. Unhappy employees give bad customer service. It's really that simple.

Good customer service is really just a by-product of what's going on inside your organization. If your employee experience is really crappy, your customer experience is going to follow. Maybe not immediately, since some leaders can lead by fear and get results for a while, but eventually it will happen. So the better the company culture is, the better the customer experience is going to be.

The bottom line is that investing in customer service is good for... well, for your bottom line. If you invest your time and resources in following these four steps, you will build a customer experience that brings you exponential returns. If you choose not to...you'll wind up paying a lot more for it, both visibly and invisibly.

The choice is yours.

CHAPTER 2

UNDER ATTACK: WHAT EVERY CEO NEEDS TO KNOW ABOUT CYBERSECURITY

By **DAN FUSCO**

Cyberattacks are destroying businesses in America. In 2021 so far alone, a company has experienced a cyberattack every 11 seconds. These companies include CNA Financial, The Florida Water System, Microsoft Exchange, and Acer Computers.

And it's not just large for-profit companies, either. In another instance, a school district in Florida was attacked with ransomware. The ransom fee was $40 million. If the school system did not pay the ransom, the identification information of all students and teachers would be released.

You might be aware of the Colonial Pipeline hack, which stopped the flow of gas to the entire east coast in the spring of 2021. Joe Blount, CEO of Colonial Pipeline, was brutally honest during an interview with NPR, saying that his company takes cybersecurity as seriously as the pipeline's physical security. However, this did not stop cybercriminals from gaining control of the pipeline. Dealing with the cyber breach was one of the most challenging experiences Joe has had while working as a leader in the industry for 39 years.

Though it only took five days to get the servers running again, Joe explained that it will take months, possibly years, to recover from the attack entirely. There are many reasons why it takes a long time to get a system fully restored. For example, when a ransomware virus is installed on a server, it embeds software in parts of the operating system which could remain dormant for years. These malicious programs, stored in remote parts of an operating system, could "wake up" and start creating havoc at any time, or simply be the back door to another external cyberattack. Therefore, companies need to rebuild their entire networks to be fully secure and ensure that malicious programs are not lurking on the network.

This kind of rebuild takes a lot of time--time when the company's systems need to be offline. And downtime can be the demise of a company. Imagine you were not able to work or run your company for five days. How would that affect your business? Do you bill hourly? If you have 50 employees and are charging by the hour for fees, the lack of revenue adds up quickly.

In addition, there are other costs associated with a ransomware attack. For instance, getting the data decryption key from the cybercriminals cost Colonial Pipeline 4.5 million dollars. Paying the ransom was a problematic choice for Joe, and the FBI cautioned him against it. Often the cybercriminals use the ransom money for other criminal acts such as terrorism. Unfortunately, this was Colonial's only way out.

Many business owners think that their business is too small for cybercriminals, that what happened to Colonial could never happen to them. I speak at many security events, and when I start to mention cybersecurity, eyes begin to glaze over because most audience members just don't think they'll ever be the victim of a cyberattack.

Sadly, they're wrong. Remember the cyberattacks that happen every 11 seconds? Many of these attacks are focused on small and medium-sized enterprises. Why? These companies are low-hanging fruit for cybercriminals. Many business owners think their firewall is good enough, or the IT guy told them the backups are running great and that the antivirus software is up to date. You would be shocked at how untrue this is and how open to attack these kinds of companies really are.

Even if those kinds of security systems are up to date, cybercriminals are far ahead of this technology. Think about it. THEY HACKED INTO THE COLONIAL PIPELINE. If they can get into the Colonial server, I am sure yours would be a walk in the park. I can't overstate this: you and your company are MUCH more vulnerable than you think, and the risk of cyberattack is as real for you as it is for Colonial, Acer, Microsoft Exchange, or that Florida school district.

Okay, enough doom and gloom. Let's assume that you understand the risk of cyberattack and are taking it seriously. You might even be losing some sleep over it. What can you do to protect your company?

Over the last 11 years, we have worked with thousands of end users, and during this time, we have created five steps that you can take today to mitigate an attack dramatically.

Step One: Protect Your Email

Emails are the number one way cybercriminals get essential information about computer systems. Unfortunately, they often send emails that are seemingly from friends and slowly, over time, without you knowing about it, gain critical information about your network. Email filters are the best way to prevent these emails from coming into your system. Look into getting an enterprise-level email filter like Mailprotector. At the time that this book is being written, Mailprotector is one of the leaders for filtering email. However, the leaders for these services can change over time, so please look at several companies before choosing one.

Step Two: Invest In Antivirus Programs

Antivirus programs are the second on the list—and you must get an antivirus that is specific to ransomware, which many programs don't address. Again, the big players often change, but SentinelOne or Huntress are excellent for slowing down an attack. I have also found that Microsoft Defender, part of the Windows Operating system, is very good for ransomware security.

The key difference to using a program like SentinelOne is that this software is designed to stop a program from running on your server. For example, a Microsoft Word document has the extension .docx. Ransomware will change that extension to .gamma. Once the extension is changed, the file will not open because it won't be able to connect to its original opening program. That file is then encrypted by the ransomware, so you cannot change the extension back. SentinelOne would notice these changes as they are being made and stop the malicious program from running; therefore, the extensions would not change. Although not foolproof, this will be a great way to slow the attack down.

Also, adding a little redundancy can never hurt, because if one security measure misses a piece of malware, another will catch it.

Step Three: Institute Zero Tolerance

With a zero-tolerance program, employees cannot install a program without the approval of an administrator. Let's say an employee goes to a rogue or unfamiliar website and is asked to download and install a plug-in. This plug-in could be benign, but it could also contain malware or ransomware. Rather than automatically being approved, the install would request approval from an administrator.

On September 20, 2020, a cybercriminal attacked a hospital chain with ransomware. It was a very unfortunate event that reduced the hospital chain to having its 90,000 workers use paper for all transactions. Can you imagine the chaos that caused? The attack risked people's lives. The ransom attack on the hospital's AKA Ryuk (linked to Russian cybercriminals), used a script that the hospital's system automatically downloaded to cause the encryption damage. A zero-tolerance program would have prevented this attack.

Step Four: Back Up Everything

Backing up data is a crucial step in recovering from an attack. There are backup programs that can back up the entire server at night. It is a great idea to have a local backup as well as an offsite backup. An offsite backup means that data is stored in a data center not associated with your network. For at least one of your backups, you will want to encrypt your backup files so they will not be compromised.

Backups aren't just great for retrieving lost files. Let's say ransomware attacked your system and encrypted your files. With good backups in place, you could just restore the entire image of the server. By restoring your data, you would not have to pay a ransom. Keep in mind that this restore would take a couple of days, and you would most likely have to rebuild your entire network. But at least you won't lose data or have to take the risky step of paying the ransom.

Of course, backups only work if you perform them regularly. Why don't massive institutions like Colonial perform frequent backups? This is literally the million-dollar question. Often backups are simply overlooked. People think their data is being backed up, but vast parts of their servers are neglected. In some cases, the scheduling for the backups is not working correctly, resulting in the backups not being performed at night. As a CEO, you should request weekly or even daily reports of your backups, then you will know if they are successful or failed.

If you want to look into different vendors for backup, I suggest Veeam (excellent for file recovery and taking system backups), Datto (an excellent local and colocation backup company), or StorageCraft. There are hundreds of vendors to choose from, some great and some—you guessed it—not so great. So please do your vetting. You should also hire an IT company to administer these programs for your company.

Step Five: Set Up 2 Factor Authentication (2 FA)

2 Factor Authentication (2 FA) is the final step in ensuring that you will not be compromised. Cybercriminals can create programs

that they can use to log into your systems. They will access your computers when you are not using them and log in with the passwords stolen from a keylogger program. (Keylogger programs record your keystrokes and are used to get into servers, desktops, and even websites like bank accounts). 2 Factor Authentication sends a code directly to your phone when an attempt is made to log into your desktop. So if the cybercriminal doesn't have your phone (which they won't), they will not be able to access your computer. A very reliable company that can support 2 FA for your company is called DUO.

Just by following these five steps (email filter, Antivirus, Zero Tolerance, Data Backup, and 2 FA), you will dramatically increase the security in your network. However, putting it all together is very tricky and can be costly. Sadly because of cost, many large corporations do not have these five systems in place; this is the main reason why they have been compromised. A ransomware hit to a company will cost them far more than setting up proper security.

Remember, cybersecurity breaches happen every 11 seconds. The damages done are in the billions, and the threats are getting worse every day. Businesses are at war with these criminals, and serious loss can happen to you personally and your business. Therefore, I encourage you to look at your IT department as an asset to your company. If done properly, you can build a fast and secure IT department that not only helps you stay protected but can help your company thrive.

CHAPTER 3

LEADING WITH R.E.A.L. VALUES

By **DAVID ANDRAS**

There are many ways to lead. You can lead from expertise, from power, from wealth, from charisma...the list goes on. I've tried most of those, and I've seen them work some of the time and fail a lot of the time.

What I've found is that the most effective way to lead is from your values. Not because values make you a leader per se, but because when people see you living your values, they are naturally drawn to follow you.

Here are the four values that have helped me grow the most in leadership. I've taken the first letter of each and dubbed them the four R.E.A.L. values. I know developing and embracing them will make your leadership as real as it has made mine!

Relationships

The first value of business leadership is relationships. You have to build genuine relationships with people--not superficial relationships where it's clear you only want to know them because they can pay you or help you or make you look good. Genuine relationships where they feel I value them and I feel they value me, where they get to know me and I get to know them, where we feel like we've been friends for ten years even if we've only known each other for two or three.

Clearly you want to build these kinds of relationships with your clients and customers, and your best customers will be the ones who build this level of relationship with you over time. But even over the lifetime of your business, the likelihood of being close friends with more than a small percentage of your clients is pretty small--especially in the industries I work in, fitness and hospitality.

So where this value is even stronger and works even better is in building relationships with your staff members. Customers literally come and go all the time in my gyms and restaurants. But quality staff members stay for years. One of the things I've been proudest of in my years of business ownership is how many of my staff have stayed with me for five or six or seven or nine years.

One of my current managers started in a gym of mine when she was 16 or 17 years old as a kids club attendant, part-time. Then she moved from kids club to working at the front desk. Then she became a front desk manager. Eventually she moved up to being the general manager of the gym, which she's been for the last several years. And now that I'm expanding into co-working spaces, she's getting ready to manage multiple gyms for me.

Now clearly this person is a fantastic worker with a great attitude and so on, but none of that would have happened if I hadn't taken the time to build a genuine professional relationship with her from the beginning. I've helped her every way I could, teaching her not only the front of the business, but the back-end as well. So she knows as much as I do, she gets my vision, and we share solid trust.

Not every staff member is going to be that clear-cut a success story. Not everyone will want to stay for years or build that strong a relationship with their boss. But you can still build genuine relationships with your employees for however long they work with you. Here are three steps to help you do that:

1.   ***Be together with them, not separate from them.***

   It's easy for the boss to give orders, but order-followers are a dime a dozen. It's harder to say hey, we're in this together and I'm going to work just as hard as you are, but that approach will make the difference between people who can't wait to jump ship and people who love to row in the same direction.

2.   ***Set clear expectations from the beginning—on both sides.***

   Earn their trust by showing them what they can expect from you, and then giving it to them every time. This will encourage them to do the same for you.

3.   ***Help them get better.***

   If you're the leader who wants to help them grow as individuals—professionally, personally, or both--they will want to help you succeed in return.

Education

I was probably 18 or 19 when I went to my first sales seminar. And it was a lot of the stuff you'd expect from a sales seminar--lots of rah rah rah, let's make a ton of money, that kind of thing. I don't even remember the specifics. But what I do remember was a question they asked everyone: what are you doing to educate yourself? Education is ongoing, the presenters said, it's not just something you do in a weekend seminar and then forget about. So what am I, teenage Dave sitting in this seminar room, doing to educate myself? How am I becoming better as a person?

That question literally changed my life. I walked out of that seminar and started reading books I hadn't even heard of before. Books like *How To Win Friends and Influence People*, *Power Positive*, and *Think and Grow Rich*—now I know everyone knows those books these days, but just imagine or remember discovering them for the first time. It was like opening a window where before there had only been a wall.

And from there it just continued. I couldn't get enough knowledge. As I moved through different jobs in restaurants and bars and entertainment and hospitality, as I shifted into fitness, as I started to move up the chain into management and ownership, I kept learning everything I could. When I became a personal trainer, I dove into every book and course and certification I could find on nutrition. You get the idea.

This value ties in closely with the third way to build relationships with your staff. Education is a fantastic way to help staff members do better work while building your relationship with them. I give my managers self-help books every quarter now. I make sure my trainers can get specific certifications that make their training the best. I help my staff members get better at customer service, at sales, at presentation skills.

This might sound like a lot of work for me to put in, and it can be. But it's worth it, for two reasons. First, by helping my staff get better, I push myself to get better too. If I don't keep educating myself, I won't be able to help them get the education they need. So to give them the best help I can, I must keep growing myself. And second, the best staff members give the best service, which makes for the happiest customers—and the happiest customers are the most loyal ones.

Achievement

If you don't set a goal and you don't try to achieve that goal, you're never going to get ahead. You're never going to push yourself. And then months or years from now you'll be wondering why you aren't where you want to be yet.

While I love big, crazy goals as much as the next person, I'm a bigger fan of progressive goals—what some people call baby steps. These are small (or at least relatively small) goals that each lead to slightly/relatively bigger goals over time, so you build confidence and momentum with each successful goal achievement.

When I first got into fitness, my goal was just to lose 10 pounds. I'd been in the restaurant industry for a while and had gotten out of shape, but when I had my first son I was like, I can't do this anymore, I've got to take better care of myself. So I decided to lose 10 pounds. And then after I lost 10, I decided to try for 15. And around the time I got to 15, I was really enjoying my new lifestyle, so I set a new goal to become a personal trainer and help other people get the results and enjoyment I was starting to get. The more I learned, the more I lost, the more I got in better shape, and the more I could help other people do the same thing.

What turned out really great about those baby steps was that they led to much, MUCH bigger steps for me later on. The gym franchise I joined as a personal trainer found out that I had management experience and asked me to oversee the trainers at one of their clubs. Then I had an opportunity to become fitness director at a larger club. Then I saw the general manager at that club was even younger than I was, and I thought okay, if he can do that, I want to do that. And I dedicated myself to learning everything there was about managing the gym—how to run the front desk, the back of the house, everything. Three months later, I was offered a general manager position. The next year the same thing happened with a regional manager position.

I'm not saying all this to brag on my achievements. I'm proud of them, sure, but the point I want to make is that each step I took and each achievement I made led me to the next one. I started super small, just wanting to get in shape again so I could play with my son. And then each achievement got a little bit bigger than the last and eventually led me to a whole new career.

The value here isn't in where the achievements got me or in thinking I'm so awesome for achieving them. The value is knowing that one baby step is its own achievement, and if you keep taking baby steps and going after the next achievement you see in front of you, you will end up somewhere truly amazing—and you'll be able to lead the people who are taking baby steps behind you on the same path.

Love

The final value is love, because if you don't love what you're doing, you'll never convince anyone you're a leader in that thing. And really, if you don't love it, why do it at all? If I don't love something, I don't do it. Doing things you don't love is just inviting everything negative into your life. And *doing* what you love will keep the positive things around even when negative things show up.

Loving what you do will keep you going even when the rest of your life is trying to beat you down. While I was building my fitness business, I was going through a divorce, my mother was dying, my house was foreclosed on, I was in the middle of a 2-year legal battle, I was broke because people I was working for were not paying me and forcing me to go on government assistance...it really felt like everything else in my life was falling apart all at the same time. I was getting knocked down every single day.

And the way I saw it, I had two choices. I could focus on all the terrible things happening in my life, or I could focus on the one thing in my life I truly loved: the work I was doing to help people get healthier. And there was a moment when I was like, you know what? I love what I do. I'm going to keep doing it. And I'm not going to worry about anything else that's facing me. It wasn't easy, but I chose to focus on love. And it got me through everything else.

There will always be obstacles, there will always be stuff in the way, there will always be parts of life that knock you down. And if you get punched down, it doesn't matter how hard you get punched down. Just keep getting back up and doing the things that you love. Those things will get you through any number of punches. And even more, they will inspire others to follow you—either to join you in the things you both love or to do more of the things that they love.

So there you have it, my four R.E.A.L values of leadership--relationships, education, achievement, and love. Embrace these values, and you will be a true leader—not just because the values help you lead, but because when you express the values and live them fully, people will be drawn to follow you.

CHAPTER 4

LEADING WITH WOMEN VETERANS

By **ELIZABETH YEO**

Have you ever googled, "veteran," "military veteran," or "U.S. Veteran?" If so, what images come up for you? For most searches, nearly all images show male veterans. Men saluting the flag, older male retirees being hailed at parades, retired or disabled male veterans in wheelchairs, or that classic image of "soldiers on a hill," just to name a few.

All of these are veterans, sure. But how many women do you see? Why did only two of the first 80 images I found in my most recent "veterans" search contain women?

Women have officially served in the U.S. military since 1901, though they played roles on the battlefield for decades prior. For example, Cathay Williams (1844–1893) was an African-American soldier who enlisted in the United States Army under the pseudonym William Cathay. She was the first Black woman to enlist, and the only documented woman to serve in the United States Army posing as a man during the American Indian Wars.

In the following years, women expanded their roles as engineers, pilots, intelligence officers (like myself), and other positions. But it wasn't until well after World War II that women were even recognized as veterans up until the *1948 Women's Armed Services Integration Act* which granted females the right to serve as permanent members of the military. Some major milestones for women in the military include:

- Attending military academies and serving on non-combat ships (1970s)

- Flying helicopters in combat and serving as military police and command officers (1980s)

- Flying planes in combat missions and serving on combat ships (1990s)

- Deploying on a submarine (2011)

- Serving as direct ground combat soldiers (2013)

- Serving in all military occupations and positions without exception (2016)

Back to the Google search. Now, I know women are still a minority group in the military, so of course you would see more images of men as veterans. But in reality, women make up about 10 percent of the total veteran population in the United States, and are the fastest-growing veteran population in the U.S. On June 2, 2020, The Census Bureau released a report showing that the number of female veterans is on the rise. Women make up about 1.7 million, or 9%, of veterans and it is projected that this number will jump to 17% by 2040.

Women who have served in the military are often referred to as "invisible veterans." There is a common misconception, or as I like to call it, the "single-story view," that combat service is a requirement for veteran status and that only men serve in combat or leadership roles within the military. That may have been the case in the past, but as of 2021, it has certainly changed.

For example, Ginger Miller, a Navy veteran, started *Women Veterans Interactive* which gained national recognition and now serves as Chair for the *VA's Minority Veterans Committee*. There are also now 7 female veterans serving in Congress. Three were just added after the midterm elections in 2020. There is also Major General Marcia Anderson, who is the highest-ranking African American woman in the Army and is responsible for their leadership programs. She takes on issues that range from sexual harassment, assault, minority discrimination, mentorship and training needs in order to increase the number of women in military leadership.

One of my favorite female-veteran stories is about Southwest Airlines pilot Tammie Jo Shults, a retired Naval Fighter Pilot who made headlines when she showed courage, calm under pressure, and "nerves of steel" while making an emergency landing after her jet blew an engine and lost a window in a flurry of shrapnel. She then demonstrated continued empathy and compassion for the passengers when she helped them deplane.

So what are the attributes that distinguish a woman veteran leader?

Here are just a few:

- *Proven strategists*

- *Courage and calm under pressure*

- *Ongoing commitment to service and the development of others*

- *Character and competence to navigate our nation through turbulent waters*

- *High tolerance for risk and high resiliency in the face of risk*

Another key characteristic of women veteran leaders is their capacity for greater empathy for their employees. This is due to their experiences in climbing the ranks in roles typically occupied by male officers, where they needed to develop immediate rapport with others, help form strong connections, and inspire confidence and commitment in those who serve with them.

And because most female veterans (including me) have deployed, meaning we lived outside the U.S., we've experienced a very unique character-building experience that creates an inner culture of tolerance, excellence, and high moral standards.

Women leave the military and enter the workforce with highly specialized leadership skills, having led, successfully, in male-dominated environments, which is not an easy feat. When it comes to women veterans in leadership roles, those who have worked in male-dominated industries or environments must take on everything men take on but have to work harder and perform better than their male counterparts in order to receive the same recognition. This requires confidence, courage, cognitive, social, and emotional intelligence, as well as, an extremely high aptitude, ability, and competency. (Not to mention a very thick skin!)

The reality is that our military service gives us valuable skills such as teamwork, confidence, independence, the ability to make good decisions in high-stress environments, and high self-efficacy, skills shared by high-performing founders at major companies worldwide. That translates well into the corporate world and entrepreneurship—which is why many women veterans become what I like to call "necessity entrepreneurs," starting businesses as a means to not only support themselves and their families but to continue their service in their communities as well.

Women veterans are also outpacing their non-veteran counterparts in terms of launching new businesses. The number of women veteran-owned businesses grew by nearly 300% between 2007 and 2012, according to the latest available U.S. Census Bureau figures (2012). Statistics also suggest that women veteran-owned businesses will impact more than just the business owner and their employees.

Supporting a women veteran-owned business will enable growth and self-sufficiency and will ultimately help build stronger families, support thriving communities, and add fuel to our nation's economy, a benefit and blessing for the entire Nation. Companies founded by women deliver twice as much revenue per dollar invested than those founded by men. Women veteran entrepreneurs create more jobs and hire more workers than our male counterparts, and women-owned businesses that generated revenues of over $1 million increased nearly 50 percent over the past decade, compared to 12 percent of all U.S. businesses.

Yet upon exiting the military, women veterans tend to face many obstacles when seeking leadership roles in the business world. This is often due to biases, not only against their gender but also because civilians many times don't understand the military mindset, environment, the skills gained, nor how to translate those skills into marketable skills for their firms. Most employers are reluctant to hire women veterans. The majority are concerned about future deployments and/or missed work, and many civilians stereotype women veterans as being too hard or tough, rigid, formal, untrainable, unadaptable, or angry and assume women veterans won't fit their company's culture.

Women veteran-owned businesses, on average, earn only seven cents for every dollar earned by male veteran-owned businesses, which indicates a lack of available resources and support. Women veterans also typically start businesses with less capital and are less likely to ask for business loans than their male counterparts.

We don't lack the skill sets, training or ability, just capital. That's why having access to mentors and networks, including other entrepreneurs, prospects, and partners is key and why many women veterans, who are coming to a new community after leaving their military assignments in other places, have more difficulty being able to establish the networks they need to succeed as entrepreneurs.

Like most small businesses, women veteran entrepreneurs struggle in transitioning from the military to civilian life, being solo operations, to hiring employees but, regardless, women veterans are distinguishing themselves as entrepreneurs with a "semper fidelis" attitude toward commitment and duty, no matter the challenges.

Military women are trained to accomplish the mission using whatever resources are available, most times our own personal finances and resources, and we often struggle in silence, never being given the opportunity to articulate what we truly need to succeed. Because many female veterans don't self-identify as veterans, the local business community assumes that women veteran-owned businesses represent a limited population. We are trained to do more with less, and oftentimes without regard or recognition, but we utilize our military training to identify problems, create solutions, and ensure those solutions are carried out effectively so that everyone benefits.

When it comes right down to it, within the military, there are several levels of leadership training depending on the level and rank achieved, as well as, training in teamwork and team building, leading and inspiring others, communication, training others, supervising, and critical thinking. Even those who served at infantry and lower levels leave the military with unique leadership skills such as briefing high-level stakeholders, developing and executing complex operations and equipment, on a multi-million dollar level, managing employees who range from highly adept to those suffering from stress-related mental and physical health conditions, and maintaining calm while managing intense crises.

Women veterans also have higher levels of college enrollment and higher levels of educational attainment than male veterans. Women veterans generally gain higher mental agility, have advanced teamwork capabilities, and significant leadership experiences and training translating into leaders with the soft skills that are more and more prioritized by companies after the "2020 Experience."

As we know, 2020 brought many issues to light and now that we are still settling into 2021, diversity and inclusion is a very "hot topic" and women veteran leaders play a vital role in this, why?

Diversity and Inclusion are about individuals that have unique experiences, backgrounds, cultures, and ideas. But as we all know, diversity doesn't automatically mean inclusion and inclusion doesn't necessarily mean that diversity has really taken place.

Consider the spectrum of skills, experiences, and perspectives that women veterans bring to the workplace. They have deep empathy and understanding of cultures and people, experienced in teamwork and leadership, and maintain the value of a strong work ethic. We know how to solve complex problems and can adapt quickly to changing circumstances and situations, calm or volatile. We have worked with cutting-edge technology and are comfortable in cross-functional environments. Many women veterans, many, bring international experience to the workplace, which is increasingly important in this 21st-century global economy.

Bottom line: women veterans, who have experienced working in male-dominated industries, are self-aware, strategic thinkers, adaptable, decisive, have proven communication and decision-making skills, and bring a global outlook and perspective, stemming from the strict and fast-paced demands of the military environment. Translating military skills such as persistence, grit, courage, and resourcefulness into the business world helps women veterans excel in leadership positions. Much like our beloved Marines, women veterans from all branches of the U.S. military have learned to improvise, adapt, and overcome in the most challenging, difficult, and life-threatening situations.

In addition to the skills and talents women veterans bring, they also provide instant ROI by helping businesses earn tax credits. Companies that hire unemployed veterans can take advantage of the *Work Opportunity Tax Credit (WOTC)*, also available to tax-exempt organizations, and after recent changes, *The Returning Heroes Tax Credit* now provides incentives of up to $5,600 for hiring unemployed veterans and, lastly, the *Wounded Warriors Tax Credit* doubles the existing Work Opportunity Tax Credit for long-term unemployed veterans with service-connected disabilities, up to $9,600.

Our intent as women veteran leaders is to always improve our environment for the betterment of all. The key is for companies to recognize these strengths and benefits. Many Fortune 50 and Fortune 500 organizations have started to do so and, hopefully, more will in time. So, as we settle into 2021, expanding our views of diversity should always include women veteran leaders. We always **R.I.S.E.** above challenges through **R**esiliency, **I**nnovation, **S**ustainability, and **E**valuation, creating lasting impact through our businesses and the communities we live in and serve.

CHAPTER 5

THE REAL SECRET TO SUCCESS: LEADING WITH HUMANITY

By **ELLIOT KALLEN**

Despite the COVID-19 pandemic, my company grew by 40% in 2020.

How?

There are some obvious answers. We offer excellent independent financial advising services. We have a sterling reputation in the San Francisco Bay Area. We have an ingenious in-house marketing team that drives potential customers to us. We work hard and dream big.

None of these answers are *wrong*, but they're not exactly right, either, because they don't get at the heart of why Prosperity Financial Group had its best year yet. [CS1]

Here's the real reason: At PFG, we understand that everything—our financial success, our growth—springs from our commitment to caring about our clients.

Does that sound wishy-washy to you? It's anything but.

No matter the industry you work in, the competition is stiff. It may be tough to hear, but many other people can offer the exact same products and services you do. I stand out from the pack not by offering different services, but by *really* caring about the well-being and success of my clients.

Their success is my success, and my success allows me to make the world a little bit better through charitable giving, and that giving energizes me to support my clients more. It's a positive feedback loop.

Care about the Person in Front of You

Even though my title is "Wealth Advisor," my job is *not* giving financial advice or selling financial products. My job is caring about people.

This might sound counterintuitive. After all, I run a financial advisory company worth $350 million. I have dedicated most of my professional life to providing exceptional financial advice to my clients and, over the years, I've been gratified to witness many of them achieve their financial goals.

But the truth of the matter is: there are *countless* financial advisors out there. And many of them are proficient in their field. They might even make better graphs and charts than me! But very few are willing and able to be your coach, your cheerleader, and your advocate. I differentiate myself from the competition by caring about the person sitting in front of me.

How do I do this? I get to know each and every client. I speak less and listen more. I ask big questions: *Who are you? What do you value?*

What are your financial goals? Then, I listen intently. Perhaps they are going through a divorce and need help navigating the next chapter of their life as a single person with just one income. Perhaps they are expecting and want to save for their child's college education. I learn about virtually every aspect of my client's life—which allows me to give them financial advice that supports every aspect of that life.

I do not reserve caring just for my clients. My world isn't divided into "my clients" and "everyone else." Just this morning, I met with a referral: a recently widowed woman. She does not have business to give to me, but I spent an hour with her. She was scared, and she felt like her life was falling apart. We talked about her finances, and I offered her concrete, actionable financial advice. That is what my work is about. Caring about people.

You may be thinking that this doesn't sound like how a financial advisor typically behaves—and you'd be right! Why do I behave so differently?

I was raised this way. My mother was an Auschwitz survivor who immigrated to the United States from Europe. My father grew up during the Great Depression in New Jersey. Around the dinner table, we talked about current events and what it means to be a good person, and I learned that part of being a good person means caring about the well-being of other people.

Growing up, my father "loaned" me out to a cousin who ran a bicycle shop. I built bicycles for him, and the most I would receive in return was lunch. Whenever family members needed help, I was expected to help them. I assisted senior neighbors by mowing their lawn or doing chores around their house. Helping others, caring about them, was just what we did.

I am no longer building bicycles for my cousin's customers. I am building wealth for the people who entrust me with their finances. But the heart of what I do—caring about people—hasn't really changed. And I can say without hesitating that, in the long run, caring is good for the bottom line. (But, if you haven't figured it out yet, I care about so much more than the bottom line!)

Meet Clients Where They Are

Since I began working as a financial advisor in 1993, I've guided my clients through a number of recessions. When the COVID pandemic hit in March 2020, I knew the world was headed for a global financial crisis. Prosperity Financial Group would need to pivot and adapt to support our clients in our new, abnormal reality.

To that end, we focused on growing what we already do best: caring about the people we serve—wherever they are. In practice, this meant two specific things to us: keeping our physical offices in San Ramon open for business and expanding our online outreach efforts.

Many financial services firms and brokerage houses closed their doors across the United States when COVID-19 arrived. They chose to meet their clients online or over the phone. But at Prosperity, we consider ourselves an essential service (and the State of California does, too). We took all the appropriate precautions to keep our clients and staff safe and continued to meet with people in our offices. While some clients preferred meeting online, others wanted to conduct important financial business in person. We have never closed our doors. Our utmost priority is to serve our clients—during the pandemic, and beyond.

Part of our work involved connecting with clients online. The pandemic touched all of our clients' lives, as well as their livelihoods. For some, the financial shock called for adjustments to their financial plans. With social distancing rules and strict stay-at home orders in place here in California, we sensed that people would spend more of their time online… and that we could connect with them there.

Even before COVID-19, we had begun growing Prosperity's online presence. Everything in business has gone digital, and the pandemic has only accelerated the global digital transformation. . By going digital, we were able to offer value—financial insights and strategies—to a broader digital audience.

Since 2020, our firm has grown rapidly—even as other companies downsized or closed their doors for good. It goes without saying that much of our success over the past year stems from adding maximum value to our clients' financial lives, leading to word-of-mouth referrals from happy clients. But part of our success stems from our willingness to pivot our business to connect with clients where they are… whether that is in person or online.

Model Humility and Lead with Good Humor

Our clients' well-being is at the heart of everything that I do. But I am not a solopreneur. At Prosperity Financial Group, we have a dozen employees, half of whom directly interface with our clients. As our company continues to flourish, we hope to grow our team with new financial advisors, along with other staff, to keep our business running smoothly. It is important to me that every single person who works for me cares about our clients to the same extent that I do.

For this reason, I care about my employees like I care about my clients. I am far from perfect, but every day I try to model humility and lead with good humor to create a workplace culture where all staff feel supported. I believe that if my employees feel cared about, then it is likelier that our clients will feel cared about, too.

Most people are uncomfortable making mistakes at work. So am I. But the reality is that, despite our best efforts on the job, errors will happen. They happen to everybody—it is a part of being human; it is a part of trying something new. I do not see mistakes as inherently bad, as they are often opportunities for improvement and professional growth. When I discover that I have made a mistake, I admit it and then actively seek a solution. It is as easy as owning it and correcting it. It costs nothing to model humility, and I find that its benefits are manifold.

We have developed a team where we can laugh at ourselves first. I like to get a head start by laughing at myself in the morning… because I make mistakes every day!

Our workplace atmosphere is fun. We work hard, but we enjoy ourselves while working. We like what we do. If an employee is not having fun, if they are not enjoying their work, then our company probably isn't a good fit for them. If one of my employees doesn't like their job, then I worry about their ability to truly serve our clients. My belief is that people who enjoy their work naturally provide better service to our existing clients and are better at connecting with prospective ones, too.

Give Back to Communities You Care About

The theme that unites my professional and personal lives is a commitment to service. I've spent my entire life looking for ways to help others. . My financial success at Prosperity Financial Group has allowed me to donate funds to charities that I believe in, like the Boys & Girls Clubs of the Diablo Valley.

The charity that is closest to my heart is A Brighter Day, a 501(c)(3) charity that I founded in 2015 in memory of my youngest son, Jake Kallen, who died from suicide at 19 years old. A Brighter Day is committed to helping teenagers and young adults understand, protect, and sustain their mental health.

For the past five years, we have hosted a charity golf tournament to increase awareness about teen mental health issues, which have skyrocketed during the pandemic. Donations go towards teens in need of therapy and counseling.

Through our annual Teen Talent Showcase, we offer a platform for teenagers to get together, experience the joy of community, and learn how to access resources for emotional support during the challenging adolescent years. I am proud to say that, just five years in, A Brighter Day has touched the lives of 2,000 teenagers and 500 parents. On my desk are letters from families that say that our work has literally saved their child's life.

Everything that we do at Prosperity Financial Group is interwoven with my work to raise awareness around adolescent suicide prevention. It is enormously meaningful and gratifying to me.

Looking Forward: Growing to $1 Billion

Every single day, my team and I talk about how to grow our firm. We have already grown 40% in 2020, but we have set our sights higher: we want to be a billion-dollar company. How do we get there? How do we grow without sacrificing quality? These are the questions that excite me and keep me engaged.

As I visualize the future and strategize about the steps that our firm must take to get there, I know one thing for sure: *caring about our clients will remain at the core of everything we do.*

If basic (yet often overlooked) values like caring about the person in front of you, meeting the client where they are, modeling humility and leading with good humor, and giving back to communities you care about are central to your company culture, then I believe that the sky's the limit.

CHAPTER 6

NEVER GIVE IN

By **JANET CHIHOCKY**

The year was 1941. The place was Harrow School in England, the Alma Mater of Winston Churchill. At the age of 14, he entered military boarding school. In October of 1941, Churchill was asked to return and offer advice to the young men about tenacity. This would be a fitting topic for the Prime Minister, as he was one that did not quit.

As written by Laurel King in 2013, *"Despite traveling thousands of miles all over the world to meet with the leaders of other nations, despite his attempts to negotiate surrender or at the very least a temporary suspension of fighting, nearly every nation of the world was waging battle against another. There were shortages of food, munitions, and oil; there was ongoing disruption in the supply channels for warring nations. Things had steadily increased from concerning, to frightening, to chaos, within the space of a few months. With so many daunting issues plaguing him, it's a small wonder that Churchill was able to deliver the speech. But, as always - and, as his speech would instruct the young men at his alma mater - not to quit."*

His delivery would cover that of a complete speech but there is a portion smack in the middle that would embronze this speech as one of his most famous, ***"Never give in, never give in, never, never, never, never - in nothing, great or small, large or petty - never give in except to convictions of honor and good sense."***

Over my 30-year career I have found that realistic and straight-forward advice stands the test of time and none better than, Never give in!

I can assure you that there will be moments throughout the life-cycle of your business that you will want to give in. You will be staring at data on screen or on a paper smack in the middle of your desk that clearly spells out that giving in should be strongly considered. If your outcome is to be the absolute best leader you can be, then there are five principles I want to share to help you stay in the game and Never give in.

1. Success is doing what God made you to do.

A few weeks ago I was at a business dinner with the owner of another company. He gleefully shared how much revenue he and his three partners were projected to bring in for the fiscal year. Eager to hear our numbers he asked me what JANSON projected for the year. I gleefully told him. Wanting to be polite after hearing my number, he said, *"maybe your margins are better than ours."* Maybe. Maybe not. I didn't care. I think our numbers are right where they need to be and the best part, no debt!

Leading JANSON is what the good Lord called me to do. I don't need to define myself by a number as I do not believe success can be found in a number. Success is doing well what you've been called to do.

I was at a breaking point shortly after 9/11 – with markets collaps-ing – my business and everything I had was about to collapse as well. It was the hardest season of my life both personally and professionally.

With the data that I faced, it clearly indicated that giving in should be strongly considered. The reality came hard and fast. It was as if my business went from enjoying blue skies and radiant sun to ominous clouds and severe thunderstorms. I can assure you that it wasn't a fun time. But just because we had entered this storm, was I going to fold my cards and run? It was for sure a tempting option.

After much prayer and confiding in friends that I knew would pray with me, I realized that JANSON was worth fighting for. During this tumultuous time, I learned some amazing lessons and unexpected deliverances that great times would have never afforded me. This season of my life and my company's life would end up being the hardest season yet it was the most transformational, as shared in my book, *"Chapter 11. Facing it? I did too."*

Today, JANSON continues to blossom within the military and defense markets where we are blessed to serve. We're successful because we're doing what we love and not wrapped up in the allurement of big revenue targets that "could" push us out of our sweet spot for how we prefer to service our customers.

In 2020 we had our largest year of charitable giving and are committed in every state where JANSON does business. We help support outreach centers and ministries that support homeless families with children. We're making a big difference and using our God-given talents and treasure for the blessing of others.

I thank God for the tough seasons for they have made us stronger, smarter, and more compassionate.

2. Set the right conditions for those that may come after you.

In my role at JANSON, I have had the honor to support some terrific leaders in the military. One of those terrific leaders was Colonel Anne Davis, whom I met during the height of the war in the mid-2000s. At the time, Anne was the Commander of an Army Depot where they produced equipment for the military.

When I met with Anne she was just as focused on positioning for Command future as on the current mission. She recognized that her Commands surge in current workload due to the current war was not likely to maintain in the outyears. Anne knew that a critical investment in market research and brand positioning would help set the conditions for uncovering new work and new partner for opportunities well into the future.

Leaders in the Military typically maintain their Command post for a few of years so the groundwork COL Davis was having put in place would be realized in the future …. many years after her tenure. The fruits of her labor would be realized under future Commanders.

As a leader, you have to look out and see what the future may look like and what the pipeline of opportunity needs to have in it. Anne could have been satisfied to ride out the boom and happily preside over the good times. But instead, she laid the groundwork for the downturn that she knew would eventually happen. For Anne it wasn't about taking the credit for the great ride her organization was having at the time, it was about setting the conditions for the future.

Conversely, I've seen the exact opposite occur as well. I have been in meetings with customers that were presented a deck of PowerPoint charts filled with unpromising data. Instead of lighting a fire, leading, and doing something about the failing situation, one guy in the meeting so confidently uttered, *"Well, this won't be my problem in 13 months, I'm retiring."*

Great leaders, like Anne, assume the role of leadership and set the positive conditions for those that may come after you.

I often connect with folks that worked with COL Anne Davis and they still, to this day, hail her as one of their best Commanders. And now we know why.

3. Own the responsibility and accountability.

When I almost lost my business back in 2003, six banks turned me down. During the meeting with bank #7, the banker sent to meet with us finally said…. we're going to help you. I was so shocked but had to ask why. I mean you get turned down by so many others I was eager to hear her rationale for committing to helping JANSON.

I posed my question to her and her response was simple: *"Janet, do you know how many people in your position come to the bank asking for money and were not willing to make one change that demonstrates they themselves are invested in doing whatever it takes to turn things around? You sat here and told me that you haven't taken a salary in eight months, mortgaged your home, depleted funds out of your 401k, and cut operating expenses by 60%. Janet…you you've done."* The banking VP could see firsthand that I was owning the responsibility of JANSON's misfortune. I didn't say those cuts were easy…frankly scary at times.

This was a time in my life when as a leader I had to accept the responsibility and be accountable for my decisions. What I have found is that most of us love the responsibility of leadership. We're given the charter to take over a P/L, manage a team of people, provided a budget and a line item for decision making. Then suddenly something unexpected happens. Every possible scenario from losing the competitive bid, to a mishap on the production line or an overpromise and under-deliver scenario. These are times that really test our leadership skills – both in terms of responsibility and accountability.

I will never forget some years back we were in the middle of a large facilities modernization project. We had just completed a massive interior renovation to the lobby and front office sitting area of a government customer. To our surprise, one of our large displays buckled thereby distorting the display which, by the way, could be seen by everyone who came into that building. This project had been smooth sailing and customer delight was incredibly high. Until this point. The General Officer had seen the buckling of the structural display and was not a happy camper.

We would later uncover that the materials we had used for that display expanded when a massive temperature change occurred in the building. Something that we were not aware of prior to commencing the project.

It wasn't longer after leadership had seen the damaged structure that I got the dreaded phone call. The once happy customer was not so happy. I could tell by his word selection and tone that this was not a good situation. Without asking a series of questions my first response was *"I'm getting on a plane to get out there and assess the situation."* Upon my arrival, the client leveraged the opportunity to share their disappointment. Sometimes I've learned it's best to just let them vent and not offer any excuses. My response was quite simple: *"Sir, that is why I am here and will not be leaving until we have developed a solution that meets your criteria."* I went on to say that it was on me for the bind we had put them in, and I would personally stay on this from correction through to completion.

While I had teams and crews that had done this work, it was my responsibility to both own it and make sure we fixed it correctly. I quickly gathered our team together and we worked multiple courses of engineering actions. Once we settled on the best option that would ensure success for the long haul, we reviewed our approach with the building engineer for his blessing.

Within 24 hours from being reprimanded by the customer I was back in his office briefing the solution and our recommended course of action. I went on to express my sincerest apologies but was confident with our solution.

My friends, to this day, that client is one of our strongest allies. He admired the responsibility and accountability that we displayed. He never had to reference the contract and belabor our responsibility because he knew we were not hiding from it or trying to find a clause in the contract that would free us from fixing it. As mentioned earlier, the root cause of the issue was a temperature variation that occurred in the building that was never told to us by the building engineers.

That said – we should have done our homework a bit better from the outset. We owned it, fixed it, and learned from it.

As Dr. Ben Carson says *"It's only a total failure if you don't learn from it."* So we purposed to learn from it and this setback eventually became a forcing function for improving and enhancing our pre-fabrication check list.

4. The Shattering of "Normal" Could be Your Biggest Opportunity for Growth

When the pandemic hit in 2020, some of our business was impacted. My mind was racing. We, like everyone else, were learning about the virus by the day and working aggressively to seal up our office suite and get everyone up and running to successfully work from home. It wasn't long before we realized that the normal as we knew it when right out the door. Shattered. Everything changed. From the way we worked, to how we showcased our products, to engaging our customers.

At JANSON, I started to notice something that I knew my guys could tackle. People still needed to sell, organizations still needed to conduct leader development and training showcases and "exhibit" their weapon systems and products. Regardless of the fact that in-person tradeshows and training events were null and void at the time, a platform needed to be provided to our customers. We needed to solve this problem.

I'll never forget, I was standing outside in my front yard on the phone with one of our technology leads we had hired a few years ago from LA. Scot was telling me that this immersive somewhat "VR type" of solution was already fast at work in the commercial markets. Question was – could we transport that technology to our market?

After months - and I mean months - of assessing technology, we debuted X3, an online virtual custom engagement world that is accessible via any mobile device, desktop, or tablet. X3 offers users the opportunity to explore virtual campuses, conduct their trainings, explore worlds within worlds, showcase technology innovations and product demos, conduct operational space planning, tour the digital twin of the actual facility that is a thousand miles from where you are in an immersive photorealistic 3D world.

We are now selling this solution to our customers because it affords them a forum for helping extend their reach and connect with their stakeholders faster, better and cheaper - any time, from anywhere.

When our "normal" was shattered, we paused and observed what was challenging our customers the most. They still had to conduct business. X3 wasn't cooked up overnight. We had months and months of testing and trials to see how we could make it work within our world – and we did!

We love being in the business of solving our customers' most pressing communications challenge and the shattering of "normal" as we knew it led us to an entire new product offering and revenue stream.

With these four principles behind you, you can stand through tough times and, as Churchill shared with those young students years ago, ***"Never give in."***

CHAPTER 7

AMPLIFY YOUR IMPACT: MAKING THE MOST OF MISSION-DRIVEN LEADERSHIP

By **JENNIFER SIMPSON**

Having a clear and compelling mission matters more than ever today, especially as organizations work more and more on complex issues that can't easily be "managed" or broken down into discrete tasks. Getting our mission right, and steering true to it, has many well-known benefits: it reduces supervision costs by pointing the team towards a clear goal, it helps attract talent that cares about the things you care about, and it makes it easier for everyone to understand how the work they do matters.

What's more, we now have years of research telling us that these very benefits are the things that motivate performance in a knowledge economy. We have clear evidence that a strong sense of team, alignment of values, and doing meaningful work actually drive employee performance and loyalty even more effectively than bonuses or incentive schemes.

Over the last few decades, many organizations have spent a lot of money for their leaders to learn mission-driven leadership. Then they've sat back expectantly, waiting for the benefits of better employee performance (and thus higher profits) to roll in.

Many of them have been disappointed.

This isn't because the leaders failed at leading from mission and purpose, though. In most cases, that part of the experiment succeeded dramatically.

The problem is, the companies' organizational systems, structures, and policies haven't kept pace with the individual insights and aspirations in the C-suite. So we have grown a whole generation of leaders who aspire to something more or different...but are left trying to apply what they have learned and come to believe inside organizations that were not designed to be led in a mission-driven way.

Here's an example of how this works (or doesn't work) in practice.

A number of years ago I worked for a large healthcare client that had just undertaken an organization-wide process of setting a bold new vision for its future. After many years providing fairly traditional insurance services, very profitably, they set out on a mission to focus more of their services on lifelong well-being--betting that focusing on keeping their clients healthier would be better for business in the long run.

This was a clear shift in the company's mission. They put a lot of time and energy into communicating the bold new intentions to the company leaders via meetings, promotional materials, and live events.

At the same time, as a public company, the organization had financial targets to meet. Recognizing that their shift in strategic priorities would create some temporary revenue gaps, they set about a cost-cutting initiative that would allow the company to transition to the new mission-driven work without going into the red. For this initiative, each leader was asked to come up with a reduced budget. And while most responded with traditional methods like layoffs and salary freezes, a senior finance leader (we'll call her Linda) got creative.

Taking the company's professed commitments to heart, Linda pulled her team together and invited them to consider how they could coordinate better or differently to cut costs in ways that were mission-aligned. Could they save money while improving customer well-being? Could they cut $1M from their budget without resorting to staffing cuts they knew would undermine the mission?

After several weeks of intensive deliberations, her team identified ways to reduce the length of a person's wait time in the call center, shorten the time it took to resolve claims, and standardize some of the technical systems used across departments to increase efficiency--changes the team projected would save over $1.5 M without having to lay anyone off. Proud of her team and their solution, Linda enthusiastically presented the approach to the executive team, who were also, initially, excited to see her bringing a larger number to the table than had been asked for.

In the weeks that followed, however, traditional methods of budgeting and reporting got in the way. Linda's innovative solution was treated as a one-time thing rather than a recurring savings effort, which removed much of its actual saving power (not to mention its connection with the long-term mission). When Linda and her team argued that their collaborative method of organizing and brain-storming could be used in other departments to save even more money, they were ignored.

Ultimately, Linda was asked to use a more traditional form of saving money and make staffing cuts. Not only was this at odds with the well-being mission, and not only did it demoralize a team that had been proud and excited to deliver a strategy that avoided the need for those cuts just a few weeks earlier, but the layoffs she was ordered to make actually delivered fewer dollars in savings to the bottom line.

In other words, the situation went from a mission-driven win-win to a mission-damaging lose-lose. The mission wasn't the problem, the systems meant to carry it out were. Examples like this are far too common as our ideals for leading in more purpose-driven ways collide with the calcified systems and outdated structures of our organizations.

Of course, systems don't exist on their own, they only persist because people create and re-create them over and over again in practice. In this case, even as the organization was setting its intention to change, some of the most senior leaders turned to familiar but harsher and less effective strategies instead of embracing new solutions that were more innovative and mission-aligned.

If we want to make the most of mission-driven leadership and achieve the full measure of impact we believe it can have, we need to move beyond developing individual leaders and look seriously at how we are organizing companies and their people to get good work done together.

Why Mission-Driven Leadership Matters

The premise behind mission-driven leadership is a good one. Rather than a small number of "smart" leaders defining goals, breaking them down into tasks, and doling them out to individuals who do what they are told, instead those leaders set a clear direction and inspire people to want to get there. The creativity and motivation this approach unlocks, especially for solving complex challenges, is far greater than any "management" approach can produce.

This sentiment was captured eloquently by Antoine de Saint Exupéry, author of *The Little Prince:* "If you want to build a ship, don't drum up the men to gather wood, divide the work and give orders. Instead, teach them to yearn for the vast and endless sea."

The premise is simple: **show people that they matter, as humans and to the organization and its mission, and they will be motivated to contribute in meaningful ways to reach shared goals.**

The first step is the most straightforward but also the one that gets overlooked or stepped over most often: **<u>Be Kind.</u> Treating people like they matter, and meaning it, turns out to be one of the most powerful motivators at a leader's disposal.** Dale Carnegie knew this over 100 years ago when he wrote his now-renowned *How to Win Friends and Influence People*, and the organizations that have taken this deeply to heart tend to find that loyalty is greater, engagement higher, and that innovation flourishes.

For organizations that have cracked the kindness code, **the next move is to go beyond "you matter" to "you matter to us."** One of the best ways to do this is to increase transparency and openness, trusting people with the information that affects them and their work. **<u>Being Open</u>**, far more than parties and company picnics, influences feelings of belonging and connectedness. Organizations that have embraced pay transparency, for example, spend less time negotiating during hiring, tend to provide more meaningful performance feedback, more regularly, and grow their teams' capacity to engage in the kinds of challenging conversations that fuel real growth.

Finally, **people want to know that their work matters to what their organization is up to.** This isn't just about "being in the know" or satisfying people's FOMO (fear of missing out). When leaders help their team members connect the meaningfulness of their individual contributions to the overall vision and mission, people can be much more agile and **<u>be adaptive</u>**. Rather than just "doing their job," they are able to make contributions that continue to steer toward a collective goal even in the face of dynamic and changing circumstances.

As the pace of change increases and market uncertainty makes detailed long-term planning more and more challenging, having people who see their roles as helping to fulfill a purpose will prove far more valuable than those who see their job as completing more narrowly defined tasks or duties.

In my earlier example, Linda took all of these principles to heart: she genuinely cared about her team and demonstrated that they mattered both to her and to the organization by openly sharing the challenge of needing to reduce costs, involving them in creative problem-solving, and engaging them in finding a solution that would serve the evolving challenges of an organization in the midst of transition. Sadly, these well-informed and well-intended efforts collided with older ways of organizing that undermined these mission-driven benefits.

Even organizations that really believe in the importance and power of mission, and are willing to invest significantly in setting clear direction and engaging individual leaders in championing it, can get in their own way if they ask leaders to operate in new ways inside of old systems.

How Old Ways of Organizing Get in the Way of Mission Potential

The mechanistic models of organizing that grew out of the industrial revolution were designed to optimize assembly-line-style work that was good at producing all manner of widgets at scale. These hierarchical, largely top-down systems were built on notions of "smart people at the top" coming up with solutions and distributing tasks to a workforce that was considered largely unskilled.

As we have moved into a more and more knowledge-based economy, these methods of management work less and less well, and even in today's manufacturing environments, we know that people work better when we take a human-first approach to leadership.

Yet too many organizations qualify their care in a way that sounds a lot like **"you matter, but…not as much as XYZ** (the bottom line, hitting your numbers, following the rules, being a team player…)." This shows up as systems with nice recruitment materials, a collection of nice "perks," and sometimes even a lot of transparency...but also a persistent set of rules that are rigid, impersonal, or contradictory.

Somewhere along the line basic human kindness got branded as "unprofessional." Leaders, Boards, and Investors allowed themselves to believe that treating employees like whole people, providing a living wage, or offering generous benefits, was at odds with being profitable. So we started managing human beings like resources and invested trillions of dollars in management technologies designed to turn people into profit.

The effect of this has been to **reduce autonomy**, inhibit decision-making, and massively increase the cost of supervision. We know that when individuals have some measure of control over how they spend their time and complete their tasks it increases engagement and fosters greater ownership. So why spend time and money on things that give people less influence and control over their own work? When the "company line" and lived experience don't match, people tend to feel inspired and encouraged initially, then demoralized and disillusioned when aspiration collides with reality.

This is made worse by day-to-day practices that communicate both subtly and overtly that **"we don't really trust you."** Many organizations still hold salaries so tightly that pay equity gets undermined, and have bonus and incentive schemes that are unclear or hard to predict.

These "management methods" lead to a feeling of arbitrariness that has team members feel at the mercy of senior leadership, tend to foster territoriality, create conditions in which people learn to "play the game" within a chain-of-command, and turn "accountability" into a kind of quid-pro-quo where employees learn to expect that "good behavior" comes with external rewards. The results not only can get economically expensive over time, but also cause employees to end up feeling a **lack of belonging**—isolated and inhibited rather than connected and committed.

The effect of this environment, then, is to create employees who **don't really know how or why their contribution matters** and so are willing to cut corners and do the bare minimum to get by. Why put in the extra effort when the best you can hope for is to get a pat on the back or a "prize" if the right person notices your efforts? The effect of all of this is that middle-layers of leadership feel disillusioned, and employees feel undervalued--all stuck in a Faustian bargain and unable to find the exit.

The double-edged sword here is that the leaders themselves often fail to recognize the paradoxes and tensions their own mission-driven leadership creates. In many cases, the leader does actually care, does truly believe in the mission, and does genuinely want to engage their team in bringing a mission to life. But despite these honorable impulses, they can't quite navigate the systems, structures, and/or people who set goals and run operations in their own company.

Believing in the power of their own good intentions, these leaders can easily fall into a sort of "benevolent dictator" mode of operating. Despite the persistence of impersonal policies and a lack of transparency due to systems and structures the company's had in place for decades, they assume the mission will magically drag or inspire everyone and everything to align with it. Then they're disappointed when their employees don't buy into the mission as much as they themselves have.

Linda and her team provide a great example of both the potential inherent in mission-driven leadership and the pitfalls of applying its methods inside organizations that haven't yet updated their systems to align with mission-related strategy.

What We Can Do to Amplify Our Impact and Make the Most of our Missions

The reasons for doing things the "old way" mostly don't exist anymore. The global workforce is more educated than ever, the internet provides access to more information than anyone can process, and the problems that groups of people need to solve together increasingly "spill over" the boundaries of any one organization.

The examples above illustrate what leaders can do to promote the autonomy, belonging, and contribution that motivates their teams: Be Kind, Be Open, Be Adaptive. To get the full benefit of this approach and amplify the impact of mission-driven leadership, the next horizon is to build systems that make it easy to treat employees like whole people.

Being Kind means not asking them to "check their identities at the door," and instead creating policies that are overtly, intentionally, and unapologetically heart-centered. When people feel seen, respected, and trusted they do great work. Connect them to the why, but give them the **autonomy** to figure out the how.

Being Open means sharing as much information as you can, then sharing a little more. Far fewer things need to be kept secret or private than we might think. Transparency can be turned into a competitive advantage. When people have access to both information and insights, they make decisions and contribute from a place of genuine commitment rather than just "punching a clock" or "ticking a box." This multiplies the brainpower working to solve your organization's most important problems, and the speed at which they can be solved. Creating a sense of **belonging** makes people want to do their best work and gives them the tools to do it.

Being Adaptive means fostering and encouraging flexibility and operating from principles rather than policies. When people can see how their **contribution** connects to the mission, they are better able to prioritize, shift gears, and evolve what they spend their time on to reach a desired shared result. People who are empowered to identify, understand, and adapt to changes, and who are motivated and inspired to do so, will always solve more complex challenges in a dynamic environment than policies will ever be able to produce.

While Linda and her team were a touch ahead of their time--early adopters on their organization's journey of transformation--over the next several years, that organization took their new mission-driven commitments to heart. Leaders and teams worked to make many meaningful changes to how work got done to foster exactly the kind of innovation and leadership that Linda had modeled from the beginning. The methods of collaborating across departments that she used to find those early savings became more widespread. Even more importantly, the mindset of using the mission as a filter for critical financial investments and decision-making became more and more common.

Yet there is more work to be done, both in Linda's company and in organizations all over the world. For large, publicly traded companies in particular, there are still heavy traditional constraints to navigate from quarterly earnings calls that favor short-term gains over long-term, mission-driven investments or sustainability. And public sector organizations are often beset by bureaucracy while non-profits are beholden to traditional funding and Board structures. More progress is needed.

The how-to manual for this new way of mobilizing people to do great work together hasn't been written yet, and that's as it should be. (After all, a policy manual on how to ditch the policy manual might be the epitome of paradox!) But I hope that the principles outlined here will inspire leaders to move beyond individual or interpersonal changes and take a meaningful look, alongside their team members, at how they organize.

In Zen Buddhism, a KOAN is a paradoxical anecdote or riddle used to help practitioners move beyond logical reasoning to reach enlightenment. I believe the principles outlined here can help us navigate this paradox at work by inspiring us to live into the promise of *Being a KOAN* by **building Kind, Open, Adaptive, Networks of people working together to reach shared goals.**

As we look at how to continue evolving our organizations to meet the challenges of a rapidly changing world, I invite other mission-driven leaders to join me in building a more inclusive world where human-first principles and a commitment to transparency and curiosity fuel our ability to amplify our impact, together.

CHAPTER 8

TELLING YOUR STORY

By **JOSÉ MANUEL DE JESÚS, MBA,**
President & CEO Quadrant Two PR

I share this collection of anecdotal and biographical memories to illustrate to you, the reader, how important telling your story is, in my humble opinion as a publicist. It is my hope that I can illustrate how telling my own story and that of my clients has permeated and made my career; and how it can help you, your clients, and business.

My days of working in the press and community-oriented media have shaped my life as a public relations practitioner and professional communicator, and has led to many campaign successes for clients, but the storytelling skills I picked up as a child from my grandmother really set the stage for me long before I got my first news gig or even attended my first journalism class.

All of the groundwork for my PR career was done in the news business. I started out wanting to be the nation's first Puerto Rican network news anchor. Boy, did that dream go down in flames - but not before I did a couple of jaunts at the news assignment desks at WPIX/CW 11 and Fox 5 in New York.

Years later, I was a freelance producer/reporter/anchor at BronxNet, a community access network in the Bronx, where I really cut my teeth as a reporter in one of the hottest news markets in the country. Even more importantly, it helped give a voice to residents of a borough of New York which often only receives blood and guts and sports coverage, yet like any other community, it has so much interesting and good community news to share. I had also made an appearance as a reporter on an old community affairs show on WPIX named Best Talk in Town with Nola Roeper, but BronxNet played a very important role in my journeymanship as a journalist, and all of the inside views of the journalism experience play a major role in my PR career.

I produced a story on earthquake faults in New York City for Best Talk on WPIX, which got some attention and was later re-tracked in the news department by my buddy and veteran reporter, Marvin Scott, when an earthquake did actually shake New York City about a year after my story aired. The story was inspired by a New York Daily News special report of the faults that run under the streets of Manhattan, which was published shortly before my piece aired.

Working the desks at WPIX and Fox gave me a background in journalism, practical application of the AP style, and I also was exposed to a plethora of publicists who called to pitch me stories each day, and sent sample releases mostly by fax and "snail mail" in those days.

These experiences, and the abilities to succinctly and skillfully pitch a story, understand the newsroom environment and culture, and know the needs of those who work in the press and media are what I believe set me apart from many other publicists out there.

At one time, I was overwhelmed by answering the sheer volume of those calls to the assignment desk myself. I think the key to PR placement success is very much contingent upon keeping the working condition of the person I am calling to pitch a client's story to in mind. This is important whether I am calling an assignment desk, a producer, or a journalist. If your business, event, or brand campaign plan calls for media relations and outreach, these skill and experience sets can be critical to success.

For the smaller entrepreneur, not only is it imperative that they actually do create marketing systems that drive sales, but they should and could involve news and public affairs coverage by:

1. Creating news and events that will get attention from the community and the press.

2. Being the best at what you do. Create a memorable first or even historic moment in your community, fill a need at a critical moment, and you will draw the attention of the press and general media.

3. Investing in creating your own media, which will grow your contacts database and drive exposure for your product, business, or image.

4. Being ready to tell your story (or that of your business or product) in a succinct, factual, and interesting manner, emphasizing its detailed strengths and accomplishments in a truthful, dignified manner.

5. Setting an ad budget. An ad budget is critical for the realistic, successful, controlled promotion of any product, business concern, or public image. Working toward a public image is an ongoing job where you can begin to manage your brand, product, or service's reputation in whatever overt, purposeful, and ethical way possible, in the social or traditional media.

My Storytelling and Malola

Most of my initial storytelling ability I owe to my grandmother, my "Malola," as was the nickname for Dolores Robles. Yes, I also learned much from observing great local reporters like Mike Taibbi, who I have long considered to be the best writer in local New York news. Others who I actually worked with like Ed Miller, Barry Cunningham, Felipe Luciano, and others are amazing orators, storytellers, and informational truth-tellers whose individual styles taught me a great deal just from observing.

But back to Malola. My beloved grandmother, was a third-grade educated "child psychologist" who drew small groups of neighbors to our kitchen table to hear her crack jokes and recount her life experiences, remains my nascent example of a great storyteller.

I was always a curious child; I asked questions about life that sometimes frightened my grandmother, although for the life of me I can't remember a single thing that I recall being scary. It was just the imagination and curiosity of a child. One day, we went to the beach and as a strong swimmer, I liked to go out a bit to deeper water to wade and swim around. Malola called me over and said, "Son, I don't like you swimming out so far." To which I responded irreverently, "No. It's ok! I can swim good, look, watch me swim."

She watched me, but I could tell she didn't like it one bit. She didn't scream at me or anything, but she knew that soon enough I would come in for a rest and some food. When I did that, she approached me with a sandwich and said, "I want to tell you something."

She went on to say, "Son, a very long time ago, the sea rose up in anger against God." *"The nerve of the sea,"* I thought. *"Who's crazy enough to get angry at God?"* So, I pressed her for more and she said, "Well the sea was up in arms because it saw and compared itself to God's other creations and concluded that it was the greatest of God's physical creations upon the Earth and that it deserved more.

"So, it demanded an audience with God, and finally, God acquiesced and said to the sea, 'Yes, it is true. You are one of, if not my greatest, most powerful natural creation upon the Earth, isn't that enough? What is it you want?' The sea answered, 'Let me swallow an inch of Earth per year?'

"God in his infinite wisdom knew that since the Earth is already largely covered in ocean water that this would not work well for the rest of the world's inhabitants, the humans and land-based animals would all drown. The Earth would eventually be completely covered by ocean water.

"In a thunderous response, God said, 'No, I will not do that, Sea.' The sea was very upset and started typhoons and blew strong and ominous winds and dark clouds throughout the Earth. 'Why, why?!'

it screamed to God, 'I am your greatest creation. You said so your-self.' God replied and tried to calm the sea down, 'Yes, it is true. You are among the greatest of all my natural creations upon the face of the planet, so I will give you something.' The sea was pleased and demanded to know, 'What, what will you give me?' God replied, 'You can swallow one person every day.'"

You can bet your bottom dollar that Malola got me thinking with that story and that I was swimming a lot closer to the shore. The story had such a profound effect upon me as a child that even now as an adult, I still recall it every time I'm near a large body of water.

I recount all of this for the benefit of those entrepreneurs out there who may choose to approach the press to request coverage of an event or store opening, etc. You better be ready to tell your story in-person, on the phone or in writing, or else you will get a generic response to get you off the phone and your story idea will not be covered. Telling a good story - even a fast "elevator pitch" version - is important. Almost as important as asking yourself the question any good publicist must ask you before they make the first call on your behalf, "What is news about this?" That's what their contacts and assignment editors will ask them, and if you or your publicist can't answer it, then coverage is highly unlikely, and you should consider strengthening your ad buy and content.

Refreshing Honesty

One story that is probably the most memorable came when I worked in politics. I was very busy handling a campaign for a major American automotive manufacturer. To date, it remains among the largest accounts I have ever managed.

I got a call from a woman who said that her father was running for Congress. She had heard of my reputation as a publicist and wanted me to run the communications for the campaign. I was very caught up in my work in the automotive sector and said so to the lady, who was very nice. I was flattered but I knew what a political campaign meant: long tiresome hours and drama.

But she said she wanted to meet me to tell me her father's story in person. Intrigued, I said 'yes.' She showed up at my home office a few hours later and that's when the conversation really got interesting. The doorbell rang. I ran downstairs to answer, and there she was, a stunningly gorgeous woman with flawlessly beautiful, mocha-colored skin. "May I trouble you for a glass of water?" she asked. I complied and offered some conversational niceties and then the business commenced.

Honestly, I was going to turn her down. I got around to asking what their budget was and she replied very matter-of-factly that it was $6,000. I said, "Oh, $6,000 a month?" She replied, "No $6,000 total for the entire campaign." She then told me, "I am my father's campaign manager and I'm a former stripper. My father is a good man who genuinely cares about the people of this borough and district, and I don't want anybody who might have seen me jiggle my tits in the past to hold it against him. We know you can help us with this campaign. Will you do it?"

I remember feeling surprised, but the honesty of her revelation (no pun intended) was so refreshing and so powerful. I had to say yes. Just to give a sense of the magnitude of billing and time, the major auto manufacturer was paying my agency a $20K+ per month retainer. I just figured I could use the notoriety and the money to hire some more people, and I did. In the end, although our candidate lost the election, we were complimented on the quality and integrity of our work by many, including the communications team for the incumbent candidate, which is a great honor. Usually, people in campaigns are so busy bashing each other, they fail to see the quality and integrity of the others' work.

We were a non-incumbent, dark horse campaign for Congress that tallied a respectable 9% of the vote. Nowhere near enough to win, but good enough to make a significant mark, a public statement, and provide a wake up call to the long-established big machine, politicians of the area.

The important takeaway for the reader here should be that she convinced me to take on her father's political campaign for Congress with the strength of his story and the refreshing honesty of hers. Stories can be powerful, and hers is a prime example.

Entertainers and Running Up on People

My work has involved celebrities on numerous occasions. Some of those assignments included work with Billy Dee Williams as the spokesperson for a woman's fragrance and personal care line campaign, Syndicated TV programming featuring the hosting talents of the late Kristoff St. John and Jasmine Guy, and The Apollo Comedy Hour among others, which featured many artists, including Biggie Smalls, Mary J. Blige, and Snoop Dogg

I worked on this and many assignments, teaming up with a long-time colleague, Kevin Derricotte. At one point, we were backstage at the Apollo and Kevin said to me, "Hey man, I got to meet with Snoop to give him the order of performers so he knows when it's his turn to get on stage. Why don't you come with me?" We walked up that winding staircase at the Apollo backstage area over to Snoop. I don't like running up on celebrities. People don't realize how taxing it can be to them.

These folks are being pushed and pulled this way and that way, and sometimes they do NOT appreciate people getting in their faces with requests for pictures and autographs and stuff like that. For a member of the public, that may be okay and understandable, but not for a PR professional. We met up with Snoop and Kevin started looking at his performance roster. Snoop could tell that I was a bit apprehensive and noticed that I was keeping a distance out of respect for his personal space. He seemed to appreciate that and he said to me, "It's alright Blood, you can get closer to me. I ain't mad at ya." The three of us got a laugh and went about our business of making sure it was a great show.

It was very telling that Snoop is an approachable guy. More importantly, this is a story I give to the celebrity-crazed among us. Do not assume it is always okay to run up to celebrities and get in their faces. They are human beings and get tired and cranky like anybody else. Approach celebrities with caution and respect because like the rest of us, these folks have stories of their own, and a right to privacy. We have a responsibility as entrepreneurs and professionals to keep this in mind.

As in some of these examples, your story must be unique in some form if you intend it to draw greater attention to yourself (as an artist, craftsman, writer, or performer), your company, product, or service.

Try to say more with less words. Make sure you get to the point quickly enough to keep it interesting, and keep an eye out for the stories that make what you represent great. Most importantly, make certain you are telling your story(ies) to the right person/people.

CHAPTER 9

BECOMING THE LEADER OF MY LIFE

By **KIMBERLEY DALY**

The science of my success was developed as a franchise consultant in 2012 when I built the first million-dollar consultancy in franchise consulting history. When I set out to achieve this million-dollar dream, I did not have a plan, nor did I know that what I was dreaming of doing would make me the number one franchise consultant in the United States of America. Thank goodness our big dreams often humble us such that we keep them to ourselves.

Had I known that what I was setting out to do had never been done, I might not have dreamed so big. But, with this million-dollar dream in my heart, I decided to focus only on what I could control, which was lead flow. I came up with the simple plan of finding one new prospect per day for an entire year. There was no magic to this number at the time. One new prospect per day seemed achievable with some effort, and it felt like a good place to start. I committed myself to this simple plan and got busy.

When I sat down at my desk every day, I did two things. First, I declared, out loud, that I had a million-dollar franchise consulting business, and second, I picked up the phone and started prospecting before I did anything else. The plan was simple. However, the execution was not always easy.

At first, I was not very good at finding a new person to talk to each day, but I did not make excuses. I kept going until I got that one new prospect. With focus and consistency, I developed skills at cold calling and prospecting, and it even became fun. Each day, I played the prospecting game. I would talk out loud to myself and call those prospects to me. As my pipeline grew and I had more people to work with, it became hard to stay committed to my goal of one prospect per day, but I resisted the urge to quit because I wanted to see what would happen if I followed through for a full year.

As my prospecting skills and pipeline continued to grow, my confidence soared! As my confidence soared, I came to work feeling abundant, excited, and expecting great things to happen. And guess what? Great things started happening!

After 12 months, I had built the largest pipeline my company had ever seen. I had helped more people say YES! to their dream to own a franchise business than any other franchise consultant in U.S. history had in one year, and I achieved my million-dollar goal. I will never forget the electrified feeling that shot through me when I added up my commissions just a few days before Christmas when I knew my year was done. I was $4.28 over that one million dollar goal. I remember sitting for a very long time in awe of this accomplishment.

This was the biggest goal I had ever set for myself, a goal so big that I did not even dare tell anyone about it. I didn't really have a plan other than to prospect consistently, but I did believe I was worth one million dollars. The magic of this moment forever changed my life, and as the story spread through franchising, I realized I had made history.

Not wanting to be a one-hit-wonder, and now knowing that all eyes were on me, I felt a lot of pressure that following year. Believe it or not, it was easier to climb to the top without a detailed plan, and when no one was watching than it was to stay on top with all eyes on me. I started the year with a lot of self-doubts. Could I repeat my million-dollar year, or was it just luck? I decided that if I had done it once, I could do it again. This time, I had numbers to study that I could use to build a more detailed plan, but remembering how fun my simple plan of one new prospect per day was, I did not want to get too bogged down with details. If I did not need those details to pave the way to the top, why did I need them to retrace that same path? Intrinsically, I knew that the magic of this achievement was in part due to the simplicity of my approach, but more importantly, the result of my belief in myself.

In 2013, I repeated a million-dollar year. After two years of million-dollar results, a few other franchise consultants started believing that they, too, could have million-dollar businesses. In 1954, Roger Bannister ran the first four-minute mile. Prior to Bannister's accomplishment, a four-minute mile was thought to be physically impossible. Roger Bannister believed it could be done, and on a cold, rainy May day, he broke more than a world record. He showed the world that nothing is impossible if you believe. His achievement stirred the running community. In the history of timed running events, no one had ever achieved a four-minute mile, but then within 46 days of Bannister's world record race, an Australian runner broke the record again. The following year, three runners broke the record in one race! Roger Bannister broke the limits of conventional thinking and made the impossible possible. His accomplishment inspired other runners to dream bigger. When my franchise consultant friends achieved their million-dollar dreams, I had my own "Roger Bannister" moment. Truly, when one person dares to dream bigger than anyone ever has and defies the odds, they change the world.

In the years since achieving this monumental goal, I have come to define what I call the "Science of my Success." The first ingredient to the formula is vision. "Where there is no vision, the people perish," Proverbs 29:18. Nothing great can ever be accomplished without vision. I knew exactly what I wanted to achieve.

The second ingredient to my success was a clear, simple plan. The first year I broke the million-dollar mark, I did not have a plan other than to find one new prospect per day. But even that simple plan made all the difference in my business and corrected for anything else that ailed my business. As I have thought about it since, having enough customers cures all that ails any business, not just mine!

The third ingredient to my success was the execution. As I said before, my plan was simple, but the execution of it was not always easy. I stayed committed. I disciplined myself to follow through, no matter what. Therefore the fourth, fifth, and sixth ingredients to my success formula were discipline, commitment, and perseverance.

After that came attitude. As my business grew, my attitude became unstoppable. I was intoxicated with my business, and everyone who met me felt my passion and belief in what I was doing, and that inspired them to their own passion and belief in themselves and their vision of success. Passion and belief must also be included in the formula to the science of my success.

As a business coach, I wanted to share what I had learned, so I took on the challenge of sharing my science of success with my candidates to see if they, too, could achieve success in their businesses and lives. Since 2013, I have shared my process with countless candidates who have gone on to pursue their dreams and have become the leader of their own lives.

You, too, can achieve your biggest goals and become the leader of your own life using this proven formula: vision, a simple plan, execution, consistency, commitment, discipline, perseverance, attitude, confidence, passion, and belief.

This list might not sound like rocket science, but these words cannot just be words. I lived the very essence of those words, and I became the person of my dreams in the process. I became the person worthy of a million-dollar business, and then I achieved the million-dollar business.

When we use these principles to achieve greatness, the most significant reward is often not in the achievement itself but in who we become during the process. My greatest achievement over the past decade is definitely the person I have become, the confidence I have built, and the lives I have changed.

Becoming the Leader of Your Own Life

To become the leader of your own life, you must start with clear, specific goals, and I want to inspire you to dream big!! You will only rise to the level of your own expectations, so it does not serve you to think small. There are infinite possibilities in the universe. When you are open, anything is possible, so just go for it. Live the life of your wildest dreams, not your smallest dreams. Dream in vivid color! Be specific about what you want to achieve. The more specific you are, the more wonder you will experience when you achieve your dreams. You will be shocked at how precise the universe is when you are precise in what you ask for.

With your big goals, you must then commit to focusing only on what you can control. This is one of the most important things I did when building my million-dollar business. When I stopped focusing on what I could not control, I stopped being frustrated or feeling lack. When I focused on what I could control, I came to work excited about what I could accomplish each day. I felt abundant! When I received more than I set out to achieve, and my cup started running over, I would giggle with glee at my good fortune.

Looking back, I see I was creating that good fortune with my positive attitude, the energy of expectancy, and an abundant mindset. Like attracts like, so you cannot experience lack when you feel abundant. God owns it all, and He wants to give it to us, but we have to obey the laws of the universe and ask, believe, and then receive. "Everything that you will ask in prayer and believe, you will receive," Matthew 21:22. You must believe it is yours before you will see it! "Faith is the substance of things hoped for, the evidence of things not seen," Hebrews 11:1. This is why you become the person worthy of your dreams, and then you achieve those dreams. When I felt abundant, even before I achieved my daily goal, I was sending out the signal that it was already mine. I was not separate from what I wanted. I was one with it. As I stayed in that state of belief, I attracted more of that state to me, and one year later, it all added up to achieving my dream!

Lastly, if you want to be the leader of your own life, hold yourself accountable. No one else can do it for you. If you say you are going to do it, then do it! Do not make excuses. Do not let yourself off the hook. If you do, you are just cheating yourself. I never stressed about not getting my one prospect if I was doing all that I could that day to make it happen. I knew that if I did my part, my efforts would eventually be rewarded because we always reap what we sow. When we do what we can in the natural, God always adds His supernatural. The more I focused on prospecting, the better I got at it, and the easier it was to manifest a candidate. I was literally calling them to me with my thoughts and actions.

When I went back and studied my numbers, I realized that I was only effective in my prospecting efforts about 80% of the time. I always gave 100%, but I did not always meet my goal. There will be many days along the road to any big goal where you are giving it your all, but you do not see anything happening. Those days matter! It is like going to the gym and lifting weights to build muscles. You cannot lift weights for only one day and expect your body will change. A strong, muscular body is the result of hundreds of workouts, many in which you do not see anything happening. The same is true for success in life. Just because you do not see anything happening right away does not mean the results are not on the way. Do not give up!

Since 2012, I have continued to use the science of my success to achieve my goals and dreams! I continue to dream big, set crazy goals, and ask for signs that I am on the right path. This year, I became an international best-selling author without even writing an entire book. I attracted this opportunity to me by declaring that I was an international best-selling author every day for one year. I declared I was an expert in my field, and my influence started growing. Today, I am recognized as an expert in my industry. I have attracted life-changing mentors and business opportunities. I receive the specific signs I ask for when I pray for confirmation. These signs do not always come right when I want them, but they seem to come right when I need them.

This past summer was challenging for many reasons. One August afternoon, I decided to get out of my office and relax in the pool. I closed my eyes and got lost in meditation. When I opened my eyes, I saw the most beautiful rainbow circling the sun directly over my house. Rainbows are a very special sign between God and me. I did not even know that a circular rainbow existed, but there it was as a sign that God was with me, watching over my house, my life, my kids, and my dreams. Some may say these signs that I speak of are just coincidences, but I do not believe in coincidences. I believe that if we ask, God always answers. We just have to open our eyes, ears and hearts to hear Him. "Then you will call upon me and come and pray to me, and I will listen to you. You will seek me and find me when you search for me with all your heart," Jeremiah 29:12-13. He longs for us to let go of our circumstances and let Him do it His way.

In my experience, when I ask Him for help, let go of the how, and just move forward in faith doing what I know to do, He always delivers on His promises, and His ways are much better than mine. "For I know the plans I have for you, declares the Lord, plans to prosper you and not to harm you, plans to give you hope and a future," Jeremiah 29:11. This is when I experience the wonder and awe of life. This is when I feel the most connected and alive! This is when I am the leader of my life, living my best life.

Truly, there are no limits to our potential, and anything is possible if we believe! If there is a dream in your heart, a dream so big that you do not even dare say it out loud, I want to inspire you to apply the science of my success. Become the leader of your own life to live your best life!

May my stories and science inspire you to become the leader of your life, and may you experience the wonder, awe, and magic of achieving your biggest dreams so that one day, you will have your own stories and science to share!

CHAPTER 10

LESSONS IN LEADERSHIP AND THE POWER OF PERSEVERANCE

By **PATRICIA BARONOWSKI-SCHNEIDER**

Perseverance is the basis of leadership.

Without the ability to endure challenges and withstand criticism, leadership is impossible. Without the strength to continue despite the shock of tragedy or the trauma of suffering, leadership is worthless. Without the power to begin anew, despite the elusiveness of victory or the hardship of defeat, power itself—the power to do and the power to lead—is pointless.

Leadership is meaningless without the ability to accept that which is hard. But leadership doesn't just mean hardening in response to the toughness of the world--in fact, it doesn't mean that at all. Leadership means the ability to meet hardship without hardening your heart in the process, because leadership also requires compassion.

Acts that test for character reveal whether someone is a leader in the first place. It is not enough to take a stand, it is not enough to inspire an audience, and it is not enough to speak words of conviction. Actions have the last word, and works are a verdict on a leader's tenure.

We have a wealth of leaders and a poverty of leadership. We have leaders in every field, from business to government, from science to technology, from education to entertainment. We have leaders who seem to know nothing but success. But we do not know if these leaders have the wisdom born of failure, the experience—the life experience—that no exam can test, no school can teach, and no teacher can instruct.

How do we know, in other words, if those in power have the power to prevail over their own failings? How do we know if those in power have the inner power to transcend the politics of the workplace or the distractions of everyday life to focus on a mission of existential importance? How do we know if those with the power to help can even help themselves—and if they can, how do we know that they will persevere enough to do it?

* * *

Leadership Lesson Number One: The Sky Is Falling

True to the spirit of the title of this section, perseverance sometimes falls from the sky.

For me, this happened literally: I actually fell out of the sky, due to a skydiving accident.

But my accident is a study in perseverance, from the moment another skydiver crashed into me to the many months—the years—involving my recovery. In rising from such a fall, in surviving such a fall, in living to rise on my own, I know what it means to persevere.

My parachute saved me, but first responders, doctors, nurses, and physical therapists rescued me. My family prayed for me, and my friends believed in me. With the help of many, alongside faith in the help of a higher power, a network of wires, from a tangle of rope and cords in a tree to strands of tungsten and steel in a hospital room, unwound. The knots released their hold, returning me to the bonds of affection.

The return was fast and slow, a distortion of time in which the images in my mind moved at a higher rate than the image before me, as my memories blurred while my body looked like it could not move. I had to learn to walk again, to talk again, to live again.

But for the help I received and the guidance I found, but for the one to whom I spoke in silence, asking for His assistance without questioning His judgment, but for the will to persevere, I would have never been whole again.

Perseverance led me to write these words. That I can write anything, that I can commit my thoughts to paper and memorialize my ideas in print, that I can do these things, that I choose to do these things is a testament to where I am.

Perseverance led me home.

* * *

A near-death experience is an extreme lesson in perseverance.

Introspection is a safer route to a similar end: self-discovery. Each discovery is universal in its theme and personal in its significance, containing general truths about humanity and relating specific truths to one human being: you. The truths may not be difficult to find, but they can be difficult to accept.

How could it not be difficult, when perception conflicts with reality, when what you believe conflicts with what you know, when what you seek conflicts with what you find?

Who among us wants to know the truth about introspection, that self-scrutiny feels like an exercise in self-loathing, that self-awareness induces mixed feelings, that pain is often what growing feels like?

Perseverance is how a leader manages the pain. Perseverance is how a leader grows, accumulating information, applying intelligence, and achieving wisdom.

Growth is no reason for a leader to complain. A good leader does not complain, period, because the effect of complaining on morale is poisonous. A good leader answers complaints, rather than compounding them, because an organization either advances in divisions or succumbs to division.

Coming together, not apart, is how an organization comes to be. If a leader cannot or will not narrow the divide, if they say bridging the divide is impossible, this person is no leader.

A leader owes an organization more than the terms of an agreement, the text of a contract, or the provisions of a deal.

If a leader is a person of integrity, the question of who owes what to whom is clear. The amount is what a leader pays in full, up to and through the completion of a project. More qualitative than quantitative, the payment is perseverance.

Forged in works, rather than a work of forgery, perseverance is how a leader renders payment. The payment maintains a leader's credit, upgrading it too. The payment is excellence by one for all, where a leader sets an example and an organization follows suit.

* * *

Leadership Lesson Number Two:
The Valley and the Mountain

Perseverance is a journey through a valley of despair, culminating in peace atop the highest mountain. The journey may be literal or metaphorical, but it is a journey just the same. The arduousness of the journey, with its deceptions and dangers, is the purpose of the journey, equipping a person with the tools—the life skills—to make the climb. Arduousness is what it takes to reach the summit.

Arduousness warrants admiration. Not the approval of opportunists or the support of cynics. Not the approbation of opponents or the sanction of critics. Not the hollowness of the insincere or the hypocrisy of the inconsiderate.

Arduousness commands respect and reinforces a leader's self-respect. How could it not, when a journey of maximum effort provides a maximalist outlook on life, when an expansive view changes how a person lives, when a new perspective changes how a person leads?

Without the weight of a personal albatross, without shouldering the weight of guilt or regret, the journey is too easy. If, on the other hand, the weight is excessive, the journey is too hard. The goal is to make leaders, not martyrs, where the journey is a testing ground, the valley a proving ground, the mountain a conquering ground.

The goal is to appreciate the miles that mark the journey, the milestones that define the journey, and the memories that highlight the journey: rejoicing in the light of a new beginning made brighter and more benignant by wisdom.

* * *

Abundant among the fortunate and attainable regardless of personal fortune, perseverance is nonetheless impossible to buy. What is purchasable is experience: the experience of having finished a journey, unbowed by risk, undaunted by fear, and undeterred by the prospect of failure.

A good leader exudes these qualities, confirming that leadership is the result of perseverance. A good leader also exudes goodness, encouraging people to improve their lives and make gentle the life of this world, beseeching them to come to understand that all life is interrelated, and beckoning them to join a journey—to journey to persevere—so they may walk into the light of greatness.

Perseverance is all these things and more, because if you have come this far you have the patience of the good and the goodness of a real professional. You also have my thanks.

Your interest in leadership is serious, given your investment in my story. In reading my story, you honor me with your time and attention. I honor you, too, by sharing my advice about the qualities you should develop.

I hope your perseverance affords you the chance to lead an organization, so you may establish a legacy equal to your ambitions and true to your talents.

May you pursue and achieve excellence, despite the trials of work or the travails of life. May you remember the reward that awaits you. May you see the light that signals your destination, delivering you to the magnificence of the view from the highest mountain.

May you persevere in your quest, and complete your journey.

CHAPTER 11

USING CONCEPTS OF MODERN WARFARE AND PHYSICS TO MAKE BETTER BUSINESS DECISIONS

By **PAUL CLAXTON**

If a business leader has to do one thing every day, it's make decisions. Some decisions are easy, simple, and clear. But most are not.

In this chapter, I will give you four principles for making better decisions in business. These principles are based on the unexpected but effective overlap of two concepts: war and physics.

Things Are Not Always What They Seem: Using Present Data For Decision Making

In 2003, I was serving as a US Marine during the invasion of Iraq. My company was outside Nasiriyah during the Battle of Nasiriyah, in the middle of the night, and in the middle of a dust storm. I was off shift, asleep on the hood of my military humvee when I heard my Assistant Gunner shout, "GET YOUR GUN, GET YOUR GUN!"

No doubt there was an imposing threat coming towards us quickly. I immediately grabbed my weapons and took cover behind our vehicle, and as I sighted in, I saw a dark silhouette (Unidentified

Person, or U.P.) approaching our team. We challenged the U.P., but between the dark, the flying sand, and the storm noise, we couldn't determine who they were or whether they were hostile.

Should we shoot at this Unidentified Person, or not? How could we even know how to make that decision?

Fortunately for my company, we didn't have to rely only on our eyes and our instincts to make this decision. We had two other things: situational awareness and present data.

Situational awareness means having an in-depth understanding of one's current situation, including the desired objective, the structure and systems one is working within, and the surrounding events that might influence one's situation. In short, situational awareness tells you what's going on around you and how those goings-on might affect you and others.

Present data is what allows you to have situational awareness: the most reliable and up-to-date information one can have about the situation they're in. And the military *lives* on present data. Military officers receive situational reports in real time—sometimes in increments of minutes--so they know as much as possible about the current state of their surroundings and what events are taking place in them. Without present data, their situational awareness is limited, and limited situational awareness gets Marines killed.

In this case, I was able to gain complete situational awareness from present data using my understanding of our objective (our unit's mission and organizational hierarchy of command), second-nature clarity of our structures and systems being used (rules of engagement/processes), and a well-rounded grasp on how the objective and the systems interacted with our current state at that time. From all of this, I was able to make a split-second decision: I decided not to shoot.

When this person finally got close enough for us to actually hear them, see them, and achieve positive identification, we realized the U.P. was actually a Marine Corps Staff Sergeant.

The Staff Sergeant had lost his way in the dust storm while looking for the bathroom area. He just left his unit to use the bathroom facilities (which were actually just dirt ditches) near the edge of our camp perimeter. On a clear night, this walk would have been easy, but in a severe dust storm it almost cost the Staff Sergeant his life.

I am thankful to this day that I did not pull that trigger, because I would have killed or seriously injured the Staff Sergeant. Based on the limited information I had, I'd made the right decision.

In business as in war, situational decisions are made in accordance with your objective, structure, and systems--your situational awareness and present data. Most of the time, you will find that businesses succeed or fail based on the absence or presence of clear objectives, structures, and systems.

Just like a business, our mind is a system that we use to make decisions in business, so we need clear mental objectives, structures, and systems as well.

Quantum Cognition: Physics For Real-Time Decision Making

So how do we collect data from the present and integrate it into our business?

Typically, when we think of big data, we think about cyberspace and big server rooms. But just as a corporation has a big server room to store all its data, we ourselves have a "server room" for storing data in our conscious and subconscious minds. This means that concepts from physics, machine learning, and supercomputing that typically get applied to server data can also be applied to mental functions like situational awareness.

With new technologies like machine learning, today corporations can better utilize their data to increase relevance and server room efficiencies, resulting in the discovery of hidden insights and automatic improvements. Just like a server room (subconscious) holds all of an entity's data, it decides when to send it to the client (our conscious).

And just as these concepts help businesses understand and leverage their data to make better decisions, they can also help you leverage YOUR data to do the same thing. *"If the body is a machine, and we learn, then we can practice machine learning too, not just build it in machines."*

The study of how humans process the information that is around them and already in their heads is called quantum cognition. You might recognize that these two words come from two different branches of science—*quantum* comes from physics while *cognition* comes from psychology. Quantum cognition essentially applies the ambiguity of quantum mechanics to the deep understanding of the mind.

Because we must manage the ambiguity and uncertainty of our lives mentally, and because we can't possibly keep records of all (or even any) of what we take in daily to the conscious mind, our minds struggle to make efficient decisions in uncertain situations. Quantum cognition allows us to make better decisions through fuller utilization of our conscious and subconscious minds by relying on present data and situational awareness.

It does this by reducing all the data stored in our conscious and subconscious mind to a lowest common denominator that our con-scious mind can easily grasp and respond to.

If we were to break this process down into steps, it would include actions like:

- Describing all current objectives in the mind, as well as any obstacles and challenges to those objectives

- Listing all supporting factors for these objectives (systems and structures)

- Prioritizing potential actions based on current structures and objectives to determine what is currently imperative and what isn't

- Forming a hypothesis of potential outcomes of those actions based on research analysis, situational evaluation, analysis of existing data, and self-reflection

- Determining the most likely outcomes of that hypothesis through the IFTTT (If This, Then That) approach

- Predicting and rejecting unlikely outcomes using the same process as above

- Reevaluating and revising priorities if only unlikely/unacceptable outcomes result from the hypothesis

The subconscious mind does all of these things automatically, in about the same time it takes an immense server to process a data set--that is, a fraction of a second. The problem is, because all of it happens at a subconscious level, these decisions tend to miss out on the truly conscious consideration that makes sure they're the right decisions in the first place.

In combat, that's all you may have time for--it's certainly all I had time for in the dust storm in Iraq. But in business, you can take the time to go through this process *consciously*. By carefully considering things like objectives, structures, systems, and likely/unlikely outcomes in your conscious mind, you can use all the data stored in your subconscious mind to inform better decisions than you could make subconsciously. This is called being in a fine-tuned state of situational awareness.

Linear And Angular Motion: How Physics Informs Quick vs. Slow Decisions

Linear motion and angular motion are additional concepts in physics that we can also use to simplify or increase the sophistication of our thought patterns.

Linear motion is exactly what it sounds like: moving forward in a direct line. It's not complicated, it doesn't take a lot of time, and it doesn't second-guess itself.

Think of a lion. A lion is one of the best hunters in nature because a lion does not overcomplicate its objective: the KILL. Lions are simple, yet so effective and powerful. Lions think in linear fashion. They eat what they kill, and because they have limited energy, if they don't make a decisive decision to kill when they have a chance, they could starve for a while. So lions don't think—they just hunt.

Linear thinking can help us make quick decisions when we get bogged down in uncertainty. Have you ever spent more than a few minutes in the cereal aisle trying to choose from the different brands? Or how about more than a few minutes staring into the menu at a restaurant? Unfortunately, many of us use this same paralyzed decision-making in our most important day-to-day business decisions.

Here are three tips to think linearly:

1. Break the decision or task down into small, simple steps or choices. Five small, simple decisions are easier to make than one big, complex decision.

2. Do the thing you're trying to do or decide on immediately. The longer you think about it, the more likely you will not do it.

3. Don't tell anyone about the task or decision before you do it. The more you talk about something you might do, the more your subconscious mind checks off the task as though

you already did it, making it harder for you to actually do it. (This is a big reason New Year's resolutions fail!)

"Constant motion towards an objective during uncertainty breeds certainty," so linear motion can help you when you're stuck and can't seem to make a decision.

But what if you have the opposite problem—you make decisions too quickly and often end up making the wrong ones?

If that's your problem, angular motion is your friend. Angular motion is the opposite of linear motion. It's indirect, thoughtful, detailed, and measured. It takes the time to examine all the factors before it moves. And often it doesn't even move directly toward an objective, but instead moves on a structure and vision that gets closer but also opens up new perspectives.

There are two ways to think angularly.

- **Spin angular.** Imagine the Earth spinning on its axis. It's not moving toward anything, instead moving around a central core point. Around that core, there is structure (like the water, atmosphere, trees, etc.) In business, this can be interpreted as developing a decision-making process around a personal or internal business purpose, where every decision is evaluated by how it serves or hinders that sole purpose.

- **Orbital angular.** This is more like the Earth orbiting around the Sun. It's constantly moving, but its motion is governed by the external forces of the Sun (vision or mission) whose powers keep it on its path while Earth continues to focus on its core (purpose). If Earth loses its structure/purpose/environment then the fact that the Earth revolves around the Sun as its mission is pointless. In business, this is developing a vision-based decision-making process where every decision is made based on its purpose and evaluated by how it serves or hinders the mission or vision.

Whichever way of thinking angularly you like better, here are three tips for doing it well:

1. Think holistically. Imagine the whole situation or picture, not just the part right in front of you. For example, put your hand one inch in front of your face, you just see your hand. Now fully extend your arm; you see the whole room and your hand!

2. Use the If This, Then That (IFTTT) approach to help visualize potential outcomes and results of your decision.

3. Start with the end in mind and consider everything that lies between there and where you are right now.

Continuous Motion And Perpetual Velocity: How Physics Informs Visionary Decisions

Purpose and vision are important to decision-making as well. Here is another way to illustrate purpose and vision and how these two concepts can work as part of a business structure. Consider this diagram:

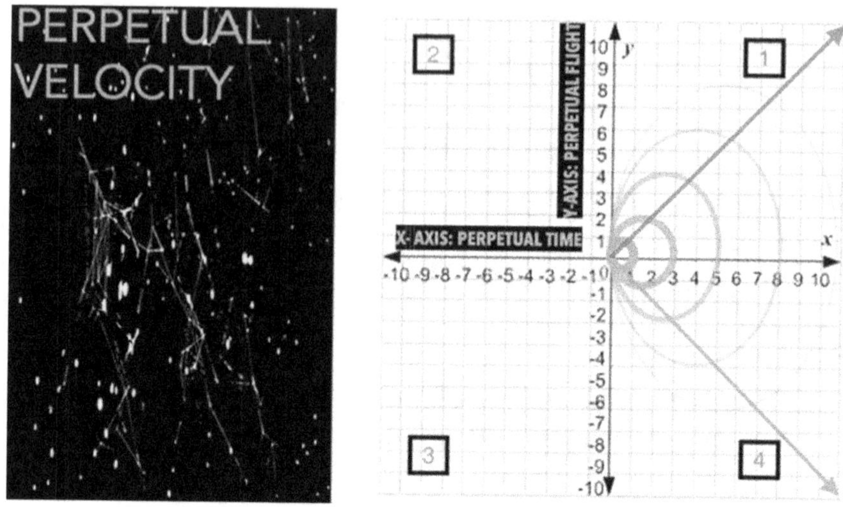

This graph is a concept of mine called perpetual velocity, which places time on the x-axis and flight (that is, up and down motion) on the y-axis. Time is a constant—it keeps going on and on and on. Flight velocity is a variable—like a plane in flight, it can change over time due to a variety of factors and decisions. The arrows on the graph represent what I call perpetual velocity in positive/up and negative/down directions, where flight is maintained or lost in contrast to time. The bubbles represent where vision can be lost over time if it's not consistently maintained.

This illustration shows how purpose and vision can impact the success or failure of your life and business.

Start at the (0,0) point at the center of the graph, the place where everything begins in existence. This is your purpose—where your business gets its start. Everything your business does gets traced back to this point. Your purpose never changes as it is the "why" behind your business, intrinsic and intangible. We can look at quadrants 2 (positive situation) and 3 (negative situation) as the situations we are born into, or the cards we are dealt in life.

No matter where you come from in life, the first decision you make about your vision is at point (0,0) on the axis or the starting purpose. How you execute your life and business over time determines if you rise into the positive (quadrant 1, where the top arrow is) or fall into the negative (quadrant 4, where the bottom arrow is).

And what determines how you make those decisions is your purpose. On the graph, the outcome of your business is determined by the constant motion you take towards your vision. The top arrow represents up motion/flight towards a positive, successful vision over perpetual time. The bottom arrow represents down motion towards a negative/crash/unsuccessful vision over perpetual time.

But because your vision can change and take many forms over time, and because not every business can maintain complete control of their visions, the best way to understand vision is to look at the bubbles.

As you can see in the graph, the bubbles show the potential fluidity of the vision, which can continue to expand over time. The bubbles also get thinner and more removed from the starting purpose over time--this represents a potential threat to the vision over time (due to delegation of decision-making, loss of centralized control from organizational growth, faulty execution, and other uncontrollable factors or force majeure).

Your vision bubble either bursts or just keeps getting bigger and bigger over time. Some bubbles pop and some don't, it depends on the consistency and fluidity of the bubble. Over time we must remain, consistent and fluid in our businesses and decision-making.

Look at Ford vs. Blockbuster Video.

Henry Ford started his motor company with a vision--and then built that company to make purposeful decisions that constantly moved toward that vision. Over 100 years later, his vision has outlasted him and his company is largely self-sustaining. Ford is a company that achieved perpetual velocity.

Blockbuster, meanwhile, lost sight of its vision sometime in the early 2000s. They failed to be fluid, reinvent themselves, and find a new vision worth following within their purpose, and so eventually they lost flight and crashed eventually losing total velocity. These days hardly anyone remembers them other than along the likes of a piece of 1990s nostalgia.

Here is the closing point: as an entrepreneur or business leader, you must keep centered on your purpose and vision throughout your decision-making processes--and remember to be willing to adjust your vision even as you keep moving towards it at all times from your purpose. The fluidity of your vision and your consistency in moving toward it will determine whether you become the top arrow or the bottom arrow. So continue to reinvent, restore, execute and polish your vision, as it can be perpetual like the pyramids in Egypt, or it can crumble like broken rock.

In Summary

In this chapter we discussed uncertainty in modern warfare, concepts of physics, consistent motion, purpose, and how all this can apply to better decision-making.

By embracing uncertainty, forming awareness, implementing concepts of physics and machine learning, and working to be constantly in motion towards an evolving vision, we can make better decisions that help us build legacies even during uncertain times and situations.

In closing, *"we all know perfection is a recipe for disaster, and you can win by an inch or a mile, but a win is a win. So, I will leave you with this final thought: there are 100 ways to do something, 99 will be good enough, and 1 is perfect, but you don't need perfection to build a great business, so pick an idea and execute with a way that is good enough."*

Thank you for reading!

CHAPTER 12

RECLAIMING OWNERSHIP OF OURSELVES

By **PETER SIEFFERT**

My personal journey began with wanting to have a better understanding of how my mind works. I had been through grade school, college, being an employee, owning a business, living, loving, experiencing life's ups and downs, and yet I had no idea how the wrinkly ball in my skull even worked. Why do I get angry in some situations and in others I am at peace? Sometimes I feel sad when the exact same situation, in a different setting, has me feel joy. Am I crazy? What's going on?

Our world is constantly providing us with input and stimuli. There is so much going on around us all the time that it's a wonder we aren't more overloaded than we are. Not only are we managing the sights, sounds, smells, tastes, and feelings (how we feel the wind blow, not the emotions we feel), we are bombarded with more complex messages as well. Messages from the news, from advertising, communications with other humans, books, television, social media, etc., all telling us what to believe, how we should live, what we should look like, what we should say, what will make us happy, what will help us fix what's broken with ourselves, on the inside and on the outside. As a result, we have come to accept certain statements and phrases as facts and realities. Simple things that mean very little in the moment are having big impacts on how we see ourselves, how we choose, and how we live.

Here's an example: "My boss **makes** me so angry!"

This statement seems like it would be right, doesn't it? Most of us have worked for a boss at one time, and some of those bosses may not have been the best. Maybe they didn't listen to our ideas. Maybe they stole our ideas and made them theirs. Maybe they enforced rules just because they liked to be in power. Whatever it was, we didn't see eye to eye with them. And it's natural for you to get angry, too! As humans, we are emotional creatures and anger is universal. There's nothing wrong with anger, it's a totally natural feeling.

But there's also something wrong with this statement: difficult bosses do not have the power to **make** us angry.

The world around us happens, i.e. bad bosses, and our minds want to make sense of it all, so we begin to make judgments and interpretations. Sometimes our minds interpret the world in a positive light. This often produces emotional responses ranging from neutral to utter joy and happiness. Sometimes our minds interpret the world in a negative light, leading to emotional responses from neutral to sadness, confusion, or anger.

The kicker is that two humans can have the exact same boss, experience the exact same treatment by that boss, and have two very different emotional responses. How can that be? If bad bosses **make** us angry, then why don't they **make** everyone angry? There is so much power in asking this question. In truth, our **interpretation** of the world around us produces the emotions we feel, not the world itself!

We see something happen, a car crash for example, and our eyes and ears absorb the information—a loud noise, two large masses of plastic, rubber, and metal colliding, smoke, steam, glass shattering, metal twisting. It all makes for an abundance of sensory input for our brains to process. As this information moves from our eyes and ears to our brains, different parts of the brain are used to make sense of the data. If we are far away, we might experience feelings of fear/concern for the drivers. Maybe we will experience anger at the negligence of one or both drivers. The list of possible feelings we may experience varies widely.

Then, if we add multiple witnesses to the scene, now we could have an exponentially different range of emotions. Maybe one person was standing very close and not paying attention. Their experience is of shock and fear for their own life. Maybe there is a first responder nearby and, due to having experienced this type of situation before, finds a sense of calm determination settle over her as she assesses the situation and determines a course of action. The point is, if you have 10 witnesses and two drivers, you have 12 different interpretations of the same event and, very likely, 12 different emotional responses.

So why does this matter? Because if the world was responsible for our emotional responses, it stands to reason that one event would produce the same response in all of us. In a moment, our unique brains, filled with unique experiences and backstories, interpret our surroundings and produce an emotional response. This means that our brains and, more specifically, our brain's interpretation of the event, is the cause of our emotional response. To put it simply, our interpretations are responsible for the anger, sadness, joy, peace, etc. we feel in any and every moment.

This sounds simple, but it's surprisingly tough to grasp. When I present this concept to an audience, almost everyone in the room agrees with and understands this concept. But when I then instruct them to "raise your hand if anyone has ever made you angry," without fail, every hand in the room goes up. In one moment, everyone is ready to own their emotions and yet, in the very next moment, they go right back to blaming their environment or another person for their upset.

The reality, if we choose to accept it, is that no one has ever "made" us angry. Oh, we have certainly been angry at people/situations/etc, but the fact remains that our own interpretations, conscious or subconscious, led to the emotional response.

As this reality begins to settle in, often people come to two different realizations. The first is usually, "Damn, I have been blaming others for my own anger and other emotions when it's not really their fault." This is often associated with a bit of guilt. At some point, though, a second realization sets in, "I don't have to react with and/or carry my emotions if I don't want to." Scientifically, if our emotions are the result of our own interpretations, I can change my emotions simply by changing my interpretations.

In concept, this is easy. In practice, it is much harder. Unless you have consistently practiced the skill, most people instantly react to certain situations; we have no real say in the moment. But what we CAN do is revisit our emotional responses and seek to understand why we reacted the way we did. Why did I get so mad when they said that? Wow, I'm so happy—what exactly is it that is causing me to feel this way? When we honestly explore these kinds of questions we can learn so much more about ourselves. Moreover, we can begin to understand what it will take to accomplish things like creating our own happiness and controlling angry reactions. If we can accept that we are responsible for the full gamut of our emotions, the possibilities are endless.

Many of us live in constant fear of losing jobs, losing friendships or loved ones, not being loved, not being liked, looking bad, being laughed at, being taken advantage of, being left out, being alone, etc.—the list goes on and on. All of these are thoughts and interpretations of situations that lead to some type of emotional response, mostly negative. Moderate, constant stress can lead to mental and emotional fatigue, lack of motivation, a reduction in our immune system's ability to fight off disease, and a host of other issues. Now we are less able to stay present and in control, which only increases the possibility that we will get triggered and have a greater number of negative emotional responses.

This a vicious cycle. The more frequently we find ourselves in this vicious cycle, the more conditioned we become to stay in it. As the famous writer, historian, and philosopher Will Durant says, "We are what we repeatedly do." Many of us are stuck in some vicious cycle or another: bad habits that impact our health, lack of patience with our loved ones, friends, or coworkers resulting in poor relationships, always giving in to other people's whims at the expense of our own time and self-fulfillment. If you dare, take a moment to reflect and see if vicious cycles exist in your life. If the answer is yes, welcome to being human.

To further complicate our journey towards emotional awareness, we are also bombarded daily with messaging that would have you believe that true happiness comes from buying a new car, having the perfect body, having tons of money, being in that perfect relationship with that perfect person... the list goes on. It. Is. All. Bullshit. Period. We need to take responsibility for our own well-being and not allow the outside world to shape our emotional experiences.

Remember, our responses are created by how we interpret the world. The new car may contribute to your happiness...until you no longer interpret it as cool or fun or exciting, or until the new model comes along and the one you own is now old (feel free to replace the word "car" with "spouse" or any other "thing" and see if you can see any difference).

The point is, we do it to ourselves. Let me repeat that: WE DO IT TO OURSELVES! This is not a moment to feel guilty about what we **_have been_** doing **_to_** ourselves! This is a moment to celebrate what we **_could be_** doing **_for_** ourselves and the world around us! We are in charge. We dictate how we feel. We dictate how we respond to those feelings and react to our world. We dictate how we choose to view our jobs, our friends, our circumstances, our loved ones and partners! As a result, we determine how our lives will go. Remember, "We are what we repeatedly do." The question becomes, what can I repeatedly do to create a different life for myself?

I think the first step is simply to accept that we are human and everything that comes with it. We were not designed to feel happy all the time, that is ludicrous! Besides, philosophically (and scientifically), would we really know joy if we didn't know sadness? Anger, sadness, joy, love, whatever we want to call the chemical reactions in our body, we all have them. And we **all** have them **all**. Before we can do anything with this glorious information about free will, we must first give ourselves permission to be human—emotional, vulnerable, reactive, responsive, needy, creative, introspective, irrational, etc. It's all good and it's all normal.

Has anyone ever said to you, while you were angry, "Don't be angry?" How well did that go? They have just revoked permission from you to be angry, i.e. human. Did that make you less angry? Not me, I just got angrier! Have you ever said to yourself, "I shouldn't feel depressed?" How did that go? Did you feel less depressed? Not me, I just got more depressed. I'm already angry/depressed and now I'm being told or telling myself that I am wrong for feeling that way. Definitely not the road to go down in order to feel any better.

What if I flipped it? What if I said to you when you were angry, "Are you being as angry as you can be? Can you crank that anger up a notch? I think you can get angrier! Let's do it!" What would happen then? I have just given you permission to be angry and to be human. Odds are, your brain would freak out! Suddenly you might pause. Your brain would say to itself, "Wait a minute, that wasn't what we were expecting. You mean it's okay to be angry? Huh, I never thought of that before."

Let's examine this further on another level. Take social interactions with friends as an example. Other people's responses to our emotions can be so predictable that we have even conditioned our own responses. Whole interactions often feel scripted out and the outcome predetermined.

How many of us have had a conversation like this one?

Me - "I am depressed."

You - "Aww, don't be depressed. What do you have to be depressed about? Your life is so great!"

Me - "Thanks, now I'm even more depressed because I know that I shouldn't feel depressed, and yet I still do."

What if you told me you were depressed and I said, from a place of support and care, "That's great! Now, are you giving yourself space and time to be as depressed as you need to be?" Again, your brain would hiccup. "Wait, it's okay that I feel depressed? This is normal? This is human? Thank goodness, I will be okay." Depression often lasts so long because we have been told that it's bad, and we are now programmed to fight it. "That which you resist, persists." Gotta love Carl Jung.

So, take a moment to recognize and acknowledge your humanness. Own that you are a thinking, feeling, and doing creature. Bask in the understanding that you are the source of your thinking, feeling, and doing. The world does not provide for you your thoughts, feelings, and actions—although they will try, time and time again, to tell you how you **_should_** think, feel, and act. Ultimately, it is your choice to either embrace what the world tells you or to tell it to pound sand. If you choose to embrace and accept your own emotions, take a deep breath, and revel in the experience of being alive. Now do this three times.

How do you feel now?

Good for you.

CHAPTER 13

PERSISTENT POWER: SEVEN WAYS WOMEN BUILD LEADERSHIP IN A MALE-DOMINATED WORLD

By **PHYLISA DEVER**

Tell me if this sounds familiar, ladies.

You're at work, doing your job and doing your best, when a customer comes in looking to buy...and only wants to talk to a man.

Or a client arrives to meet with you...and assumes you're the secretary for the person they're here to meet with.

Or even one of your own employees comes in with a problem... and wants to talk to a man about it, and gives you attitude when they have to talk to you instead.

That last one is the one I always get, because my husband and I own our business together. And there are always one or two employees—male employees, of course—who want to go to my husband when there are problems. Especially HR and accounting-related problems. When they know I'm in charge of HR and accounting, and have known since I hired them.

I don't need to tell you how hard it can be to lead as a woman in a world of men. Y'all already know.

So instead I'm going to share with you the seven steps that have helped me overcome that difficulty. I've discovered and developed these over the last twenty-plus years of building and co-owning businesses, and I've found they help me not only lead my employees, but also lead myself.

Stay Focused

As women today, we multitask a lot. We're entrepreneurs and business leaders, sure, but we're also mothers, wives, grandmothers, and sisters. We're often caregivers, too--I take care of my elderly mother, as do many of my friends with their older relatives. Some, like me, are active in our church ministries. We wear a lot of hats and don't always get to choose when we switch between them.

The problem with multitasking is that it makes it too easy to start a lot of things and never finish any of them. The way to fix that is to practice staying focused on the task at hand. Finish the thing in front of you before you start the next one.

It's not easy, but if you build it up into a habit, staying focused will serve you so well. I'm fortunate now to have an assistant, and one of her main jobs is to tell me when I'm getting off track or distracted and need to focus better!

But for years I was the person who told myself that, and it's paid off in more ways than I can count.

Be The Calmest Person In The Room

It's really hard to lead effectively when you're upset. When you're upset, it's easy to say things you don't want to say, things that might hurt the other person. And very few people, especially men, will follow a leader who hurts them in moments of anger.

With the employees who are disrespectful toward me, I have learned to be quiet until the situation has calmed down, rather than jump in and mirror the other person's frustration or anger with my own. Sometimes I don't even respond to them in the moment, instead taking a few hours to think through the situation alone first.

This way, when we come back together we're able to communicate calmly rather than yelling over each other. And even difficult employees appreciate the leadership of someone who's willing to stay calm when they themselves can't or won't.

Speak For Yourself

This can definitely mean knowing and holding your boundaries, but here I'm using it in a slightly different way. When you do need to bring up a difficult subject or resolve a problem (say, with a male employee who would prefer to talk to your husband), don't try to speak for them. Instead, speak for yourself.

Specifically, I like to use "I" statements instead of "you" statements. You may be familiar with this idea already, but in case it's new, I'll give an example. Instead of saying "you did that wrong," I would say "I feel like that wasn't right," and talk about why I feel that way. Instead of accusing, I share a perspective backed by observation.

This was a tough one for me to learn because I have a military background, and the military isn't known for softening up their feedback! But over time I discovered that even difficult male employees who will react defensively to a "you" statement will often receive an "I" statement with more open consideration.

Own Your Authority

I mentioned earlier that my husband and I co-own our business. What I didn't mention was that all the financials are in my name. So if there's a problem with a budget or if something is off with our tax return and the IRS comes calling, that's on me. So when a financial issue comes up, I know that I have full authority over that issue, and I have learned to own that authority.

For example, one of the male employees I mentioned above, who travels frequently for his role, once rented a much larger vehicle than the company typically approves our workers renting. (The vehicle was, perhaps unsurprisingly, a sizable pickup truck.) When he turned in his receipts for reimbursement, I called him in to discuss the much-higher-than-expected car rental bill, and I made sure he didn't just go and talk to my husband instead of me.

I used some of the other methods on this list to make sure it didn't turn into a shouting match, but I also didn't let this employee ignore me or get away with giving me any attitude. He was in my territory, on my turf, and in order to lead him, I needed to ensure he knew I was still in charge. You can do this, too.

Be Your Own Best Cheerleader

You may be fortunate enough to have other people in your life or career who will encourage you right now, but there will be times in your life when the only person encouraging you is you.

When I was in the military, my platoon sergeant blocked my well-deserved promotion because I wouldn't have sex with him. I was alone and had no recourse. No one listened to me. No one supported my cause. No one encouraged me, either to fight for my promotion or to get out of the military. I had to encourage myself because no one else was going to.

At first that started small, with little affirmations I would repeat to help myself keep going. My favorite was from Paul's letter to the Philippians in the Bible, "I can do all things through Christ who strengthens me." Over time I found many more quotations that inspired me and helped me build confidence. I've also found listening to energizing and uplifting music can help me feel more encouraged.

As I eventually left the military and began my journey as a business owner, I found that the more I accomplished, the better I was able to encourage myself and the more confidence I felt. Celebrating achievement, even in small steps, is a great path to becoming your own biggest fan.

Let Your Principles Guide You

Do you have principles you live by? I believe every woman should.

As an active woman of Christian faith, I find many of my principles in the Bible. Many women I know prefer to find their principles in other books or faiths, or in their own minds, and that's fine with me. But what's interesting is how often the same principles show up across many of our lives despite our finding them in different places. As the Bible says, there is nothing new under the sun.

Take the principle of philanthropy, for instance. I've known many leaders who live by this principle, who use the wealth they generate to give to others and who believe that the giving enriches them even further. There's a scripture specific to this principle, in the Book of Luke, that essentially says what you give will be given back to you in even fuller measure than you've given it. Some of the leaders I know embrace philanthropy and charity because of that scripture. Others have never read it, but still know and live by the same idea.

It doesn't matter where your principles come from, as long as you meditate on them regularly and allow them to guide your life. Meditating on my principles every day turned my life around, took me from being a broke, homeless single mother to owning four businesses and being married to my wonderful husband, and helped me become the leader I am today.

Never Give Up

All of these steps are important, but I think this one is the most vital. Never give up. No matter how hard or how bad you think it is, no matter how harshly you're being treated, never give up. Never stop pushing toward your dream or your passion, and you will get there in time.

When you run into challenges now, I urge you to stay committed no matter what. If you have to reevaluate your goals, that's okay. If you need to create an action plan or find a better solution to whatever problem you're facing, that's fine. If you're starting to get burned out and you need to take a break and recharge, that's okay too. But don't lose the passion and don't let the challenges convince you to give up.

Not only will this persistent power help you get where you want to go, it will also teach you how to be patient. And patience is more important than ever in today's instantaneous world. Patience allows the processes you're doing (like these seven steps) to do their work. Patience helps you become the leader you want to be, because that won't happen over the weekend. And patience helps you lead the people who might not think they want to follow you.

Speaking of that, remember Pickup Truck Guy? I was ready to fire him, both for his overspending and for how he talked to me. But I decided not to do it right away, to be patient with the situation for a while longer and see how it worked out.

A few days later, this employee came into my office and apologized for how he'd spoken to me. He told me about some difficult things going on in his life at the moment. And he shared that he didn't always feel like I trusted him—something I could tell it took a lot for him to admit. We ended up having a very productive conversation, where I explained why the financial accountability was so strict and that it wasn't personal to him. We also found common ground in our faith—it turned out he was a dedicated Christian, too.

(This employee no longer works for me and my husband, but the way he left turned out much more harmoniously than I thought it would. He moved on without anger or drama, and my husband and I were happy to give him a solid reference for his next job. We never became friends, but he became more willing to follow me and I got more comfortable leading him.)

These seven steps are the keys to women's leadership in a male-dominated world. I hope that by reading them here, you can save yourself the years of effort and struggle it took me to discover and develop them. I hope they help you skip over making the mistakes that I made. And I hope they help you turn your life around if that's what you need right now--that's what they did for me.

Blessings,

Phylisa Dever

CHAPTER 14

THE DISCONNECT BETWEEN BUSINESS LEADERSHIP AND SUCCESS

By **ROMAN TSAROVSKY**

For centuries business has been what drives our culture. First, it was the simple barter system. I have this and I want that, I'll trade you.

Then came simple forms of currency that allowed us to give the idea of value for something for something else, acting as an intermediary in transactions.

For example: take this printed paper I have and give me a car, a house, a boat, some land, etc.

While we use printed paper or fiat money as an example, anything can act as a currency. Indeed, at one point, salt was a form of currency.

And, throughout its evolution, many ideas on how to drive business growth in size, revenue, and credibility have been taught to the masses.

Some ideas are confusing, some are unbelievably simple yet effective, but they all lead with the fundamental principles you will learn here.

It's not rocket science to start and scale a business. It's really about paying attention to what people have been asking for throughout history and giving it to them. Reading between the lines if you will.

The major problem is, many of us love to complicate things and make it far harder on ourselves than it needs to be. And that's where the huge disconnect between business leadership and success has grown. This results in smart and hardworking entrepreneurs closing the doors on their dreams year after year.

In my experience, there are four fundamental things for being a leader and/or a business owner. If someone told me these things when I was starting out, it would have drastically helped me become more successful far sooner than by learning the hard way.

Successful Business Leadership Isn't A Secret

Everything in life starts with a structure. Business is no different. Every successful business has a core structure they function on.

Yes, they have unique selling propositions and things that make their product more or less unique, which the client may love or hate. But every business at its core operates on major principles, and the business owner has burned them square into their mind.

We're going to get to these fundamentals in just a moment, but let's look at one very important and influential brand of the past decade and see if we can recognize a key element of their success.

Apple has one of the most cult-like followings in electronics (laptops, phones, music, and now television). They seem to know exactly what customers want and how to present the product in such a way that people camp outside stores across the country for a product that often costs as much as someone's rent.

Why?

For starters, they have a clear structure on how they run their business. The owners understand the three sub-categories that define a solid business structure.

The same goes for Disney, Microsoft, and Amazon. They know something that other business leaders seem to think is some kind of a secret.

Well, it's not a secret. Here's a peek behind the curtain and as we go further into this idea we will flesh it all out in greater detail.

Let's dig a little deeper into each one of these areas of business leadership so we can focus on how each one personally can change your life in business and even other areas that require clear communication, expectations management, and problem-solving.

The first core fundamental part of successful business leadership is structure.

What Successful Business Leaders are Doing that You're Not

When I say structure it's not simply having a business model or plan. It's what all business leaders include in their decisions when dealing with customers and clients. There are three sub-categories that can't be ignored.

1. Customer Service
2. Product
3. Price

Customer service is perhaps the most important. Product is second, and last is price. If you're surprised that price is the least important, think of the price of any Apple product.

If you look at any successful business or well-known brand, they've had these three things at the forefront and in this order.

For example:

Apple has amazing customer service. When visiting one of their locations, a specialist will dedicate time to personally work with you one-on-one. That makes you feel important. No matter the problem they will solve it.

Their products are high quality and arguably at the forefront of their respective industry. Although their prices are high, people look past them because the other two major leadership structures create enough value to outweigh the cost.

Even though Apple is significantly more expensive compared to its competitors, it's not overly pricey. They're not charging $30,000 for a computer. They're charging $1,200, $2,000, or $3,000 for a computer.

What About Relationships?

The customer is always right. Remember that quote. It's hard to forget because it's so powerful, that's why the first core idea of business leadership is built on customer service.

But what about the next tip. What do other business leaders that make money hand over fist do that you don't? If you're as sharp as I think you are, you probably guessed it. It's managing relationships like a savant.

That's right, when you run a business there is no room for mistakes between your staff, clients, or customers.

The second core pillar of successful business leadership is Relationships.

And there are two sub-categories we will address later on.

They are:

1. Communication
2. Expectation Management

Too often there are disconnects in communication. Some weren't clear on what they needed to do, or a part of the process was not explained properly with a confirmation that all parties involved understood things.

Throughout any type of business venture, you are always dealing with other people, even if it's internal, external, as a true leader you are a communicator.

You allow people to follow you and you need to provide an eco-system that allows them to succeed under you.

Successful leaders know they work for the people. The people don't work for you.

That's the difference between a leader and a boss. A boss orders people around, and has people work for them.

A leader works for the people, empowers them, goes to battle, side-by-side with them—and leads them to the successful execution of whatever they're trying to execute. That takes excellent communication and all of that has to do with building a relationship.

Expectation management sounds straightforward enough, doesn't it?

But it's one of the major disconnects in business leadership.

If you have communication, but people don't have the right expectations, people are going to be hurt. They're going to have expectations that are let down. And it's just going to provide a very unhealthy experience.

Imagine it the other way around. If you have expectations, but you don't have good communication, then you don't have fair expectations. As a leader of your business, how can you expect things to be done properly if you don't communicate what you expect?

This is going to lead to disappointment, which is going to lead to hard feelings, anger, and problems in the relationship. Not to mention problems with trust and execution.

So as a leader, you need to communicate frequently either through instruction or receiving instruction or feedback.

Won't I Lose Clients if I Say No?

A lot of people have huge reasons why they don't say no to business. They want to prove themselves. They think they can do it. They want to make the other person happy. They don't want to disappoint for whatever the reason is. They need the money.

The list goes on and on.

But in the long run, it does more damage than good. And It's going to cause you agony if you don't learn to say no.

Learn to say no.

This is the third fundamental rule to becoming a successful leader and managing a scalable and profitable business.

If you struggle here it's okay. You're not alone. I did it, and learned the hard way. A lot of people—business owners—have a very, very bad ability of not knowing when and how to say no. Simply put, knowing yourself, being very honest with yourself. And most importantly, being honest with the people is totally fine.

It is very, very important to say no, because if you don't say no and later on, it turns out to be a no, then it damages core fundamental step number two. And your communication and expectations are just not there. Then you will have destroyed the reputation of yourself, your business, your product or service, and whatever it has been. And that stuff is not recoverable.

There will be more examples that follow but this rule often is the hardest to master so understanding this more deeply will help ease your fears. We will go further on how to do this later in the book.

The Leadership Approach to Solving Problems

I live by this in full honesty. It can be the hardest thing you possibly do. It may be harder for you than learning to say no. But nonetheless, great leaders are masters at this and we want you to take this last core concept and add it to your everyday approach to business asap.

In any type of situation, any type of problem, There is one question you want to ask yourself. That one question is, can you do something about the situation?

If the answer's no, then you should not worry about it. And in every single conceivable way, no matter how hard you think it might be, how selfish it might be.

But if there is nothing you can do about the situation, you should not worry about the situation.

But if you answer yes, then you must do the work. It's not easy, but it is very simple. Most of the time we already know what has to be done. Great leaders know how to make the problem manageable. This means doing something if something has to be done.

But instead, you take that energy and use it on something else you can control or solve. That could be improving a process, working on a new product, or something else to enhance your business.

Problem-solving has to do with finding core reasons the problem exists, then really digging down deep and finding out if you can actually make a change that will solve the problem or if you have to let it go.

It's Time You Build the Business You Deserve

The Four Ideas discussed in this chapter have drastically improved my success as a leader, a business owner, and an entrepreneur.

Structure, relationships, boundaries, and problem-solving are the top four things that will catapult you to becoming the leader, employer, partner, or friend you want to be, and improve every single aspect of your life, the same way it's helped me.

The disconnect between business leadership and success has become wider than ever before and, if it continues, will falsely promote that it's overly hard to build and sustain a business in today's ever-changing world.

The truth, however, is that if you work hard at learning these fundamental ideas, you will build what you could only dream of in a shorter time than you ever thought imaginable.

If you take the time to study every successful leader and business making noise today. You will easily find these fundamentals at the base of the business supporting it as it continues to provide massive gains for both its owners and customers.

CHAPTER 15

THE RIGHT PEOPLE

By **RUSSELL G. LUCE, RFC, LUTCF, FIC**

Have you thought about what comes next for your business after you've moved on? I'm 57 years old, a pretty average age for an advisor. But the vast majority of advisors don't have succession plans. Earlier this year, I was in a T-bone car accident that easily could have killed me had fortune not been on my side that day. So if something happens to me, what happens to our clients?

The uncertainty of that question is one of the reasons I make sure there are excellent people around me. Too often, the instinct is to always be the loudest voice in the room or to make yourself seem irreplaceable. I believe instead that a leader should always be looking for their replacement and helping them grow into someone who can step in at a moment's notice.

In order to lead and train the right people, you must first surround yourself with the right people.

Even after 30 years in my field, I would never claim to be the smartest one in the room. That's something that I'm not only not embarrassed to say, but a fact I believe has propelled me to any success I enjoy today. No one is going to always have all the answers in a business, so it's crucial to surround yourself with the right people.

Now let's talk about how to find, connect with, and lead these people.

1. Look for drive, not talent

On my first day in corporate America as a new director of sales for a firm, the VP of sales didn't allow me to talk to anyone while I was setting up my office. Instead, I was called in to meet all of the staff at the same time – this was my chance to show that I was the new sheriff in town. The first thing I said was, "What does success mean to you?" After some vague, fluffy answers, I asked instead what a great sales goal was for the year. We took three months off the timeline to account for vacation and divided the target number by 40 weeks. I told my new staff that if they didn't feel they could commit to reaching that goal, they could hand me their resignation by the end of the day. Then I held a 15-minute meeting with each of them to come up with a base plan for how to hit the target. Five employees out of the 20 on the team left the company that day. By the end of the year, just five of those original team members were left.

What made those five special? Were they that much more talented as salespeople than the others, or better read with fancier degrees? Not in the slightest, but a few traits stuck out in all of them. For one, they were trainable and coachable. Secondly, they had the drive. Like me, they didn't want to just be average. I like to say that if you act like just an employee, you're always going to be an employee. That's a fine lifestyle for a lot of people – to just clock in and out of their nine-to-five job, collect their paycheck, and then go have a beer on the couch at home. But if you want to be a leader and own a business at some point, you have to make a company's success your business. That drive is what separated the team members who made it through the tough love of that first year on the sales team.

2. Value street smarts over book smarts

"Surround yourself with people who are smarter than you" is a common phrase, and I certainly live by it. But what does it actually mean? I don't believe it has anything to do with college degrees or test scores. Oftentimes we'll have new employees who blew us away in their interviews. They sounded great, they looked great on paper, but once they're out in the real world, it's a different story. I saw it all the time in my former career as a police officer. New officers would come out of the academy with all the wind at their back and everything going great. But when they first get into a situation where a gun is pointed at them, you learn what they're truly made of. It's the same in business. I don't want a team member to just tell me what they're going to do, I want them to show me. I should've been born in Missouri!

So, it's much more about street smarts than book smarts. How can you handle a difficult situation? How do you solve a problem? As leaders, we take a scenario, find the right tools, and go after the solution to the situation. The way you do that is by hiring the right people, and a lot of that is trial and error. Sometimes we hire the right people, and sometimes we don't. One thing I try to do in hiring is focus on peoples' strengths rather than their weaknesses. We all have our personal pitfalls, but we can work to improve, especially if the drive is there.

Something else I appreciate in an employee and in a leader is the ability to lead by example. In the football offseason, teams hold workouts for extra preparation that are only mandatory for younger players. Why is it still important for the veterans to show up? They already know the playbook, the routes to run, and the strategy to implement. But as I heard one analyst and former football player describe it, the workouts are about much more than that. They offer a chance for more experienced players to get to know the newcomers as individuals, and for the young players to see the veterans as their leaders. If you don't know the people who make up your team and their strengths, you're going to be lost trying to lead them.

3. Stop giving orders and start asking questions

For most of my 30 years in the financial advising industry, I haven't been a great listener. But in the past few years Van Mueller, one of my mentors who's been in the business longer than I have, has given me some life-changing advice: stop telling people things and start asking them questions instead. If you ask someone the right questions, you're going to lead them down the right path. But the key difference is that they're going to go down it themselves, rather than you pushing them down it.

So what are the right questions to ask people? You've got to find out what makes them tick. What are their goals? Why do they get up every day? These questions accomplish a few important things. First, they help your team members envision greater goals than just ticking tasks off of a checklist each day. If they feel like they have a purpose, one that you care about and value, they're going to be more of a self-starter. Second, it helps you better understand your team and its needs. Whether you're leading a group of people in the sales division or leading a company that sells widgets, you need to know what motivates them. The same can be said for outward-facing relationships as well. If we don't get to know our clients, it doesn't matter what we advise them to do. They won't trust us and our expertise won't make a difference.

Asking questions will certainly help you when you're not in a leadership role as well. Business can be cutthroat, but you might be surprised at how many people are willing to mentor you along the way if you just make the small step of reaching out to them. I've been so lucky to have been guided by some of the best in my industry. It's not because I came into the field with the most impressive financial advising credentials, but because I made it clear to them that I was willing to do absolutely whatever it took to be successful in this business.

One of my sons, Ronald Luce, graduated college with an accounting degree, but his passion lies more in the numbers of sports. Trying to break into the sports podcasting industry isn't easy, but his dedication shines through. I'm constantly in awe of what comes out of his mind. He's been coached under some of the greats, and more importantly, he knows how to ask the right questions in order to improve his craft.

There are two things I can't coach people on: drive and ethics. But if you have both of those going for you, I can teach you the sales.

4. Aim to make a difference

If you can make a difference in someone else's life, then you'll have a good day. Even when I'm down, I always try to make somebody laugh, or take water out of my pity bucket and help them out. To me, that consideration for others is what separates a leader from just another employee. I've been so lucky to have been mentored by some great people over the years, and now it's my responsibility to try to pass some of that learning and experience on. Because if you're a leader whose end goal isn't just personal gain, but making a difference, then you have to bring those around you up to a higher level.

I'm so proud of my other son, 36-year-old Staff Sergeant James R Luce, a master gunner in the U.S. Army. He's such an incredible leader that every single one of his troops would die for him. I get choked up just thinking about that sacrifice and what it says about him as a leader. And it doesn't just apply to the military. In business, you want people to feel like you made their life better when they consult with you or buy your product. If that's not what you're in business for, then why be in it at all?

There are plenty of easy excuses to just play your role and plug in your slots and call it a day without making an impact on much of anyone. I also believe that anyone can make a difference in any field, not just business. Whether you're a window washer or a janitor or a CEO, you have an opportunity every day to make someone else's day better. If you can do that, you're going to be successful as a leader and as a person.

I've learned so much from those around me over the years. My business partner Tara De Maria-Nolan changed the passion I have for my business. Mike Pickerill has taught me how to dream bigger. I learned from Tony Golden how to be more humble. Van taught me how to ask questions and listen to others rather than give orders. Countless others have taught me other vital lessons.

If you're afraid to have people that are better than you or smarter than you on your team, your team is never going anywhere. But if you embrace bringing the right people onto your team and leading them the right way, you will build both a team and a business that will be proud to carry on your mission after you're done.

CHAPTER 16

LEADERSHIP – THE PREQUEL

By **SHARIF ALMAMUN**

What is leadership? Is it the ability to direct people in a precise manner? Is it having the kind of salesmanship where you can talk anyone into doing anything? Or maybe, is it possessing enough charisma to deliver that one speech that can make someone jump off a skyscraper?

Dr. King's leadership gave a presence of greatness and something bigger than we thought we could dream of. President Obama's speeches gave us hope. Mahatma Gandhi dared the people of India to live free. Every exceptional leader had at least one noteworthy quality and carried an irresistible aura.

These are exceptional leaders who came to touch billions of people. But did these leaders just wake up extraordinary, or did they too have to struggle to achieve greatness? What if you are not a natural-born leader, do you still have hope?

Before Sylvester Stallone became Rocky and Nelson Mandela became the first black president of South Africa, before Elon Musk started Tesla or Steve Jobs grew Apple to the global tech giant it is today, they too had to go through their own journeys. None of them were born the leaders they became. Yes, we all may have some raw talents, but to truly shine we need discipline, patience, persistence, and a little luck. We may never become an Elon Musk or a Steve Jobs, but we all have our own journey and path to overcome.

Here are six keys I have found helpful in taking that journey to leadership.

Build A Routine

Do you know why McDonald's is so successful? There are many mom-and-pop burger joints that have way better burgers than McDonald's, so why aren't they all multibillion-dollar corporations?

When you walk into a McDonald's, you know exactly what you are going to get. When someone buys a McDonald's franchise, they follow the exact same procedures. In other words, McDonald's has built a clear, easy-to-follow routine. Following this routine, and requiring all their franchise owners to follow it, has made McDonald's the successful company it is today.

Successful leaders embrace routines.

When I wake up in the morning, I spend some time listening to positive affirmations or motivational speakers to shake off any negative vibe that I wake up with, then I spend the next 15-20 minutes just reading or meditating. Some days, I just sit on my deck staring at trees and wonder about the beauty of the creation. My nightly routine includes putting electronic devices away 2 hours before I hit the bed, doing a few sit-ups, drinking a cup of caffeine-free tea, and doing some light reading.

You don't have to adopt my exact routine. In fact, while studying other people's morning and evening routines can be helpful for inspiration, it's best to figure out the routine that works best for you.

It does not have to be a rigid routine, either. Make it your own. Make it in a way that is comfortable for you. It will take some time but once you start to feel comfortable, do it for 3 days, then a week, and tweak it if you need to. Then when you are ready, do it for 40 days. If you miss a day, don't sweat it and come right back to it. It usually takes 40 days to make something your habit and once it becomes a habit, trust me no one will have to ask you to do it. We owe it to ourselves to give us that hour or so each day to keep ourselves focused and to appreciate ourselves.

Master Your Mind

An average person has around 6,000 thoughts per day.

Let that sink in for a second.

If you're awake for 16 hours a day, that's one new and distinct thought about every ten seconds you're awake.

Being able to channel your thoughts and stay focused is one of the biggest challenges that most humans face. Anyone who has achieved greatness has been able to bring their focus to a singular point in time, ignoring outside noise. Mastering your mind takes tremendous hard work and focus. We spend years learning to multi-task, so undoing it is never easy.

I started to practice mastering my mind by intentionally picking a task and giving myself 5 minutes to only think about that task. Let's say you are driving, turn off your music and allow yourself to only focus on driving for 5 minutes. You will see how many thoughts come to your mind but as they come, observe your thoughts, and let them pass. Recognize the thoughts that appear, you don't have to fight them, and then just move right back to that one task. As you practice, you will see your ability to concentrate will improve tremendously over the years.

Master your mind because it is yours. It should listen to you and not the other way around.

Communicate Clearly

Have you heard Morgan Freeman speak? I'm sure you have--his voice is one of the most recognizable in the world. His slow, deep, deliberate speech is always clear and easy to understand, not to mention warm and welcoming.

But he didn't just start out that way. Did you know that he took voice coaching and practiced for years to find his pace, rhythm, and true voice? This is true of most famous actors and performers, particularly the ones known for their speaking voices.

Clear communication isn't a talent, it's a skill. It can be learned and practiced and mastered. Over the years, I have gotten pretty good at giving my sales speech, but I still was afraid of presenting in front of a large crowd. I ended up joining a local toastmaster to give me the push that I needed. Practice speaking in front of people or start by speaking in front of a mirror.

On the other side of the coin, clear communication means being as good a listener as you are a speaker.

As you grow into a leader or run your own business, you will want peers and clients to feel that you hear them. You want your partner to feel heard when they talk to you. And you want to be able to listen to your mentors.

The challenge is that no one teaches us how to listen. Parents always tell us to be quiet, but do they ever tell us how to? When has ever someone told you how to truly listen? For those like me who love to talk, you need to work on listening more. When someone starts to talk, I focus on my body language (body facing them), eye contact (looking at them), and my focus (really listen without constantly distracting myself with surroundings). I also count to 3 when they pause, to make sure they've finished speaking before I respond. I strongly recommend this practice! Don't worry about answering immediately, you will notice that when you take time before you speak, people's attention grows and their focus changes.

Build A Healthy Relationship With Yourself

Throughout my 30s, when I had just begun to work on myself to improve my own flaws and learn from my past mistakes, I watched myself failing to build long-term relationships and evaluated myself repeatedly. It forced me to change. One of my most redeemable qualities is the openness to learn new things. Admittedly, sometimes I resisted. However, because I have always been a true student, I usually accepted the changes.

Unfortunately, I can be naïve. I tend to get excited too easily and can jump into things. There were plenty of regrettable situations that came out of that naiveness, but it also taught me to be cautious and to trust my gut over the years. I saw a therapist, read books, started meditation, listened to motivational tapes, and started to focus on understanding myself better.

I realized that I need to know myself well before I can know others. As my company started to grow and I improved my relationship skills, I started to notice that more and more people wanted to work with me. I built some long-term relationships with both small and large companies. I started to look for mentors. I realized that you must first put your intention out in the world, then do the work before you can expect results.

As I was manifesting mentors and preparing myself for them, the right people started to appear. I found a mentor in IT Strategy work in a person who I worked with a decade ago. Because of our relationship, we managed half a dozen (some budgeted for 100 M+) projects together since then. I found another mentor company that just happened to be looking for a company with exactly our skill sets. This led to us starting a Joint Venture and an SBA (Small Business Association) approved mentor-protégé relationship that helped us mature significantly faster.

I would have missed those opportunities if I did not take the time to build a good relationship with myself over the years. Work on improving yourself to be a better person so you attract the right kind of people because our lives are all about relationships.

Practice Failing

You may have heard the story of a man who lost his job at the age of 32. Shortly after that, he was defeated in a run for his state legislature. He then started a business, which failed. His girlfriend died two years later, which led him to have a nervous breakdown. Two years after that, he began a series of political campaigns, including two nominations to the US House of Representatives, two more for the US Senate, and one for the Vice President of the US. Over twenty years, he was defeated in every single election.

But the next campaign he ran for, he won. And that campaign was the presidential election of 1860.

As you've probably figured out by now, or possibly knew already, the man in the story is Abraham Lincoln, generally considered one of the top two or three presidents in US history (if not number one). Lincoln's many failures prepared him to succeed.

What if failed attempts were seen as practicing success? It would relieve people from the pressure of needing life to be perfect.

Did you learn to walk on your first attempt? Did your parents put you on a time-out after your second attempt to walk? Why is it that you are not encouraged the same way when you come home with a bad grade or when an employee can't deliver his/her project on time? You must accept that you will fail in life, that you will be disappointed, that you will get hurt in the process of finding love, that you will lose when you compete for a project, that you will definitely lose when you try to lead a team. The sooner you accept the fact that you will lose at times, the sooner you can start the process of winning.

You don't need to win every project you compete for, you don't have to hear yes from the first girl or boy you talk to and you don't have to give up just because one of your business ideas failed.

Accept failing as part of your winning strategy because when you are searching for love, you only need one right person to say yes. When it's about business, you can create a million-dollar business with only a few strong relationships and when you are trying to change the world, you really need a small number of the right people on your ship to help you steer. So accept failure as a step toward your next win.

Let Your Purpose Find You

Every leader talks about finding your purpose and the thing that moves you. Some find that purpose at an early age like the Dalai Lama or Dr. King. Some wait for decades to respond to their calling like Mother Theresa or Mahatma Gandhi. For some of us, the reason just shows up out of nowhere.

Mine showed up weighing 5 lb 12 ounces in 2001 when I was 25 years old. I wanted the flexibility and financial stability to never miss a moment of my daughter's life which led me to start a business. As she grew older, I wanted to be a better person to set the right example for her.

Through that process, I found my path and my true calling. I never lacked motivation and even in my worst days because I could never quit on her. My path may have changed, I may have endured extreme lows, but my purpose is so strong that it means my existence. When your true purpose comes, you will know. It's just like love. No one has to tell you what it is, you just know it.

Let your purpose find you, don't rush the process. And if you continue to stay a student and master the leadership skills, you have already decided to lead your life and when your true calling shows up, you too may rise up like Gandhi or Dr. King and lead a generation to its freedom.

CHAPTER 17

KIDS FINTECH: THE TIME IS NOW TO HELP OUR CHILDREN MAKE THEIR OWN ONLINE PURCHASES

By SUZANNE E. KECMER

In the swift global move from cashless to contactless payments that society has experienced during the COVID-19 pandemic, children, for the most part, have been left out of the conversation. Which is odd, isn't it? Kids are the ones who know the most about the internet these days, especially as forced remote schooling has made them even savvier than they were before.

Why isn't it conceivable that a 5-year-old child could buy the newest toys, books, and videos directly on Disney+ after watching his favorite animated television series? Why shouldn't a 6-year-old elementary student pay for her school lunch at check-out? Why can't a 12-year-old adolescent purchase merchandise while playing League of Legends?

Any of these scenarios could easily happen through each of these children's own mobile devices via a family wallet app or other pre-approved online spending platform. There could be a payment button option on every retailer's checkout screen, enabled by e-commerce platforms, to process child-specific transactions. Raising financially responsible children in this age of increased digital interconnectivity could be part of their overall education and development, instead of an economic privilege or social taboo.

But that's not what's happened so far. Instead, both parents and tech companies have been reticent to focus on next-generation payment technologies specifically aimed at children (age 13 and below).

This has largely been due to several different factors:

- Parents historically have maintained bank account balances for children and handled pre-approval of spending, saving, and allowance personally, so kids are required to constantly bombard parents with requests for cash or credit cards rather than making their own purchase decisions

- Parents have also been uncomfortable with the price of children's debit cards, reinforcing the above situation

- Commercial entities have had no ability to legally collect children's purchase data, so companies haven't been able to effectively sell directly to children

- Banks have artificially set the minimum age for account set-up at 14 years old, so younger children can't open their own accounts

But all of these factors are quickly decreasing in their effectiveness. Seamless integration between virtual and physical environments is quickly advancing in sophistication. This renders current parental delay tactics practically useless, such as application monitoring and handing a plastic credit card to your child at the point of sale, particularly as increasingly younger children interact and embrace technology for everyday tasks with fluidity. Furthermore, software platforms are collecting and forecasting user information at a faster pace than ever before imagined, thereby gaining greater influence over children to shape behaviors.

I have been witnessing these market gaps first-hand while advising REGO Payment Architectures, Inc. (REGO) within my investment banking practice for a few years now. REGO has been developing a next-generation, two-sided payment platform, as well as an all-digital family wallet, specifically to allow children of any age to make purchases online independently.

The key to this new technology is the ability for the child's parent to pre-define all the guardrails the child may experience while banking or shopping online, to feel comfortable that their concerns will be addressed and their children will be safe.

REGO's platform has three defining factors that set it apart from other platforms and make it specifically safe for children's purchases:

1. ***The ability to define data control settings from parent to child***

REGO approaches this problem using a master account to dictate purchase rules to subaccounts via a hierarchical architecture—REGO has patent-protected this data control methodology. This approach adheres to data flow and privacy policy requirements specifically outlined for COPPA (Children's Online Privacy Protection Act) compliance.

2. *The ability to obscure the child's transaction and personal identification*

Authenticating and validating the identity of the actual user on the internet maintains one of the most challenging cybersecurity problems. REGO has solved this hard problem by masking user data and maintaining separate identity and financial data flows—REGO has also patent-protected this attribution methodology. As a result, REGO is able to verify the age of the internet user throughout the transaction lifecycle on its platform.

3. *The ability to disseminate transactional data on minors while remaining COPPA/GDPR compliant and maintaining strict data security*

According to law, COPPA/GDPR (General Data Protection Regulation) compliant data can be disseminated, used, and sold. This data includes the geolocation of the purchase and the age range of the buyer on an anonymized basis. Without extreme data control features, such as those in the REGO platform, any lesser data precision will be less useful for sellers and less safe for buyers.

What does a COPPA/GDPR compliant payment platform really mean? In short, COPPA, for example, in the United States was enacted in 1998 and became effective in 2000 by the Federal Trade Commission (FTC) to protect the privacy of children aged 13 and younger. As of this publishing date, there is proposed legislation to expand the age range of children covered under the law and strengthen federal oversight of internet services aimed at kids to be moved up to 16 years old. The FTC has approved seven Safe Harbor Programs (TRUSTe, ESRB, CARU, Aristotle, PRIVO, kidSAFE, and iKeepSafe) to encourage self-regulation—a modern-day good housekeeping seal of approval, if you will. REGO uses PRIVO, to ensure both FTC compliance and maximum safety for child purchasers using their platform.

I recently had a discussion with Claire Quinn, Chief Privacy Officer of PRIVO, to see where she thought COPPA and GDPR compliance was headed specifically for the global payments industry. Ms. Quinn said, "Children under 16 make up more than 40% of internet users, are tech-savvy, and want to make purchases. The industry has recognized a need to allow children to buy online while putting the parent in control. However, there are inherent privacy and security risks in relation to the personal data collected and processed to provide these services."

We also discussed the security complexities of payment solutions versus other applications. She explained, "Pocket money and money management apps must undergo rigorous privacy and security processes to protect children and families. A simple gameplay app and a fintech app would undergo the same process of review for regulatory compliance, for example, under the Children's Online Privacy Protection Act (COPPA). However, the fintech app brings greater risk and therefore robust controls are needed which wouldn't be required for basic gameplay."

I suspect as more COPPA and GDPR compliant payment solutions come to market, we will see the Safe Harbor Program mature. Ms. Quinn believes, "The privacy landscape is changing globally with new legislation emerging that focuses on protections for teens as well as younger children. This is ever more vital as new technology develops and brings more complex and sophisticated digital experiences and interactions."

I think one immediate modification that needs to be made within the certification program is to move away from a uniform seal approach to a more nuanced recognition program that differentiates platforms with more sophisticated security controls.

For example, Exhibit 1 below shows the technology stack of a COPPA-compliant all-digital family wallet. The wallet allows for payment using a mobile device via digital versions of a credit card and debit card that are stored within a wallet app on the mobile device. In this case, the parent and child are interacting within the same wallet via privileges set by the parent. Transactions not permitted by the parent (e.g. defined at the store or product type level) will not be executed.

Exhibit 1: *Example of a Next-Generation Digital Family Wallet Tech Stack*

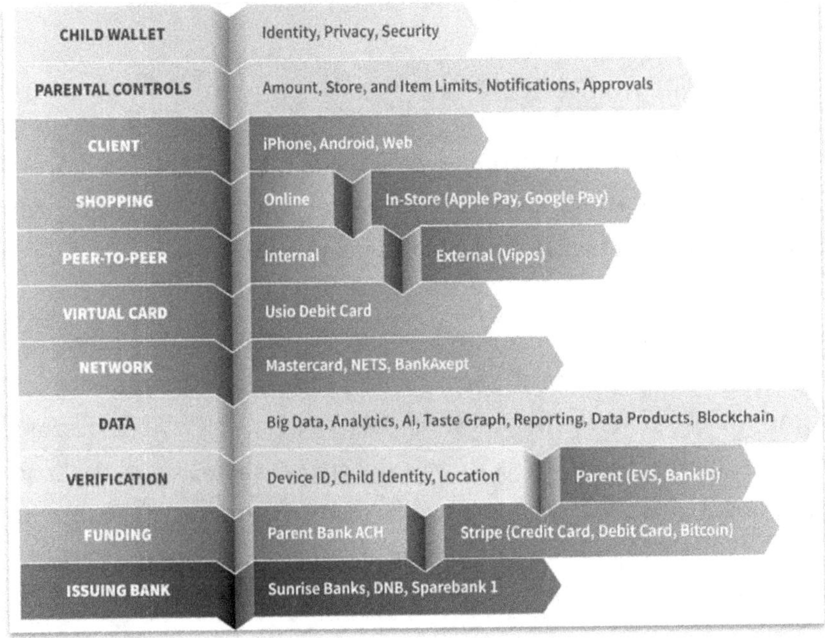

Source: One Kiln Marketing, LLC

The rigor to achieve COPPA and GDPR certifications by PRIVO of an all-digital payment system includes demonstration within this enterprise architecture of:

- Alignment with the Minors Trust Framework, created by PRIVO under the National Institute of Standards and Technology (NIST) for Trusted Identities in Cyberspace, which provides a secure method for sharing identity credentials, specifically between children's identity and parental consent, across technical, legal and operational policies.

- No direct commercial advertisement to children.

- Resulting data collection and dissemination that excludes user identity and obscures user age.

These are the sort of advanced technology solutions that need to be adopted. Safety hygiene awareness campaigns and government regulations have been largely ineffective in safeguarding data privacy and cybersecurity—regardless of user age.

Business leaders and parents/guardians need to address the core problem of baking security and privacy requirements into commercial software development from the start. This is crucial to prepare future generations to co-exist successfully in a global society that places such a growing emphasis on the power of the internet of things while largely ignoring most, if not all, cybersecurity and privacy risks.

Moreover, the FTC is enforcing violations concerning children's online privacy. Previous significant violations have included websites, apps, games, and other online services that did not follow the proper policies to obtain verifiable consent from a parent or guardian prior to collecting information from a child. Currently, failing to comply with COPPA results in fines of approximately $43,000 per privacy violation per child, and fines have reached a record $170 million for one institution. GDPR compliance is being equally enforced. Significant attention must be paid to compliance with these regulations, particularly as the volume of child online activity is anticipated to increase dramatically.

There are many immediate steps that business leaders and parents/guardians can do now to implement advanced payment solutions for children that protect their identity and data.

What Business Leaders Can Do Now

1. Implement enterprise-wide learning modules that pertain to the current status, violations, and evolution of the global regulatory environment– e.g. COPPA, GDPR, CCPA (California Consumer Privacy Act).   Given the broad impact of these measures, all divisions within an organization need to understand how these regulations impact their direct role.

2. Ensure new product development incorporates security from the initial design phase—including a holistic approach across information technology, physical and personal security. Pay particular attention to identity and consent measures, as well as metrics.

3. Invest in enterprise architectures that allow for spiral development in order to incorporate leap-ahead security measures to be in front of advanced cybersecurity threats– as these threats are constantly changing. Persistent outreach to the offensive cyber community is paramount for situational awareness of the threat environment.

4. Seek highly scalable solutions that can be embedded within the existing enterprise architecture and information technology backbone of an organization. These types of platforms may provide an umbrella regulatory compliance solution and may be able to house existing non-compliant applications. This would offer speed to market and tangible cost benefits.

5. Organizations, such as retailers and financial services providers, should review the collection and storage aspects of their data management policy. The purpose here is to ensure segregation—no intermingling—of minor children's data repositories from other data repositories.

6. Join the FTC-approved COPPA Safe Harbor Program to use your organization's children's privacy compliance as a marketing discriminator. Increase visibility of regulatory compliance to consumers, partners, and colleagues.

7. Appoint senior executives and Board members who are directly responsible for security, privacy, and data management. Visibility of these executives is important.

8. Pursue government relations efforts to understand the evolution of the regulatory environment and potential business implications.

9. Initiate recruitment efforts of security, privacy, and data management professionals from non-traditional fields. Outside the box thinking may be an important element for growth.

10. Seek technology partners that scale and are well-positioned to address next-generation, advanced requirements.

What Parents/Guardians Can Do Now

1. Seek applications and other software programs (e.g. games) that showcase safe harbor seals and other compliance metrics.

2. Look for payment solutions that do not expose children's personal identifiable information (i.e. photographs, credit card numbers, social security numbers).

3. Try to find solutions in which the parent/guardian opt-in to the utility features of the payment platform and thus, have control over the data collection and dissemination. Meaning, platforms that allow the parent/guardian to define the shopping experience and other guardrails during internet usage and to dictate how (if at all) the platform provider may disseminate the child's user experience and behavioral trend data.

4. Keep abreast of the current regulatory environment, as it is evolving.

5. Many children's payment solutions today incorporate financial education tools that can help navigate the increasingly successful and safe adoption by children of "smart" products within the household.

Enabling children to transact online will position the global payments industry to meet the robust demand of this very savvy internet generation (digital natives)—who after all, will not be kids forever and will demand these types of advanced security measures as a lifelong baseline.

CHAPTER 18

THE ALF WAY

By SUZANNE ST. JOHN-CRANE

In 2016, I took a leap of faith. After having built two television stations in the bay area, I left a twenty-four-year career in public television to dive headfirst into American Leadership Forum (ALF), a forty-year-old leadership and human development organization whose Silicon Valley Chapter was looking for a new CEO. Three years earlier, ALF had recruited me into their year-long Fellows program, where I was immersed in relationship building and candid conversations – or "dialogues" as we learned to call them – with classmates who were leaders in their respective private, public, and non-profit fields. The experience pushed me and taught me several valuable lessons – not the least of which was that I needed to devote more time, not less, to my own human development. I've found that dedicating time to human development is not indulgent; quite the contrary, it is an investment in the networks I move within.

Becoming the CEO of ALF forced me to live the tenets of "The ALF Way," aiming to be a living example of how we move through life as leaders, and more importantly, as human citizens in our own communities.

The work brings me in regular contact with leaders who, despite their considerable achievements, are surprised by how much learning they have left to do. In 2018, I was having a conversation with a prominent entrepreneur who was considering whether to say yes to the ALF Fellows experience. "Suzanne, I've started and sold companies. I coach CEOs who are household names. Why do I need a class on leadership?" To which I responded, "Well, this is less about becoming a better leader and more about being a better human being."

To which he quickly admitted, "Oh, I need help with that."

Don't we all? The entrepreneur said "Yes" to the experience, grew a lot as he went through it, and ultimately became an ambassador for it to other private sector executives.

I invite you to put what you know on pause about leadership, human behavior, and problem solving for a moment, and instead to consider a series of concepts and practices that we've observed at ALF over our forty-year journey, which have transformed how many of us have shown up personally, professionally and in community. Some are common sense, but not common practice. Others are so, so simple to understand, but wrenching to implement. What we've learned over the decades is that these practices, if we commit to them as our north star, can get us unstuck, and thus making better decisions within the spheres we influence.

What's your 7-minute story?

In the beginning of every ALF Fellows experience, we create a confidential space where Fellows are asked to share with their 25+ classmates, in seven minutes, about the people and experiences that made them who they are. We often point out that you can come to the room with your "A" story or your "B" story. Your A story is an elongated LinkedIn profile. Your B story is the messy reality, complete with trauma, failures, stories of survival, and nagging regrets. The idea here is that we leave our ego and job title at the door and meet each other as people first. If we can know each other deeply, and commit to prioritizing our mutual humanity first, it can provide us with a new lens for our decision-making, centered in empathy and inclusion.

It never ceases to amaze me how much the Fellows' relationships change from when they walk into the room to tell their stories to when they exit as peers, — not with titles or accomplishments, but as fighters and survivors of this complex human experience. The CEO who was homeless as a kid. The attorney who had a gun pulled on him by police for "driving while black." The government official whose sister was murdered as a child. The weight we carry as humans is extraordinary and built into our DNA and our decision making.

Can we see each other for our history and privilege, for the roadblocks we've overcome and the guilt we may feel for easing into positions of power unearned? Can we truly embrace all that makes us? I challenge you to consider that everyone has a 7-minute story and to lead with love and empathy as you encounter and connect with them. (Reminder: Empathy is the key ingredient for building better widgets, teams, and communities.)

Being Mindful

Internationally renowned Scientist and Meditation Teacher Jon Kabat Zinn brought the practice of mindfulness into the mainstream about fifty years ago, creating Mindfulness-Based Stress Reduction (MBSR) after having studied Zen Buddhism teachers such as Philip Kapleau, Thich Nhat Hanh, and Seung Sahn.

The Mayo Clinic describes mindfulness as "a type of meditation in which you focus on being intensely aware of what you're sensing and feeling in the moment, without interpretation or judgment." Mindfulness can be a part of your everyday routine, even while eating, walking, driving, and working.

About ten years ago, ALF incorporated a mindfulness practice into its Fellows curriculum and eventually into the culture of the organization itself. "Um, how does lying on the floor doing a body scan make me a better leader again?" I am sometimes asked. Oh, let me count the ways. Building the muscle of presencing allows us to fully hear and thoughtfully pause before responding. That's how it impacts our leadership. By training ourselves to be still and aware, we can better navigate the incessant waves of tasks, urgencies, and critical decisions with clarity and purpose.

I first witnessed this practice without knowing it as a live television director-in-training. My guru Robert had worked for decades in the field, sharing that the most successful directors are actually the calmest, aware of the placement of all ten camera angles as they thoughtfully switch between them, sewing images together completely on the fly. I, on the other hand, started off as a gum-chewing, chain-smoking protégé, gripping the wheel for dear life as I barked at camera people to zoom in, pan left, and tilt up. I would watch the pros, keeping their voices low, commanding cameras while simultaneously slipping in directions to the audio engineer to fade mics. Their focus was uncanny, like a conductor directing an orchestra--focused on the music, yet intently aware of every individual instrument at all times. I took note and traded cigarettes for deep breathing.

Practicing mindfulness as a leader allows us to have our finger on the pulse of our emotions at any given time, being acutely aware of our tension and reaction in any given moment. We're able to feel the room and give space for others. We can hear completely and respond meaningfully – even if our response is short and sweet. I dare you to practice being extremely aware of one thing at a time.

Dialogue vs. Diatribe

Old habits die hard. We come to conversations with lived experiences that influence our beliefs and assumptions about others. It's only human. Many of us assume a role, perhaps unconsciously, in conversations. We bring the idea, we buck the idea, we pick a side, or play the quiet observer. ALF is big on dialogue, inviting us to show up to the conversation with a courageous frame. If ever there was a time in human history that we needed to have better conversations across differences, it's right now. Try this on for size, if the topic and circumstances allow.

Pay attention to who's invited and who's *not* at the table. Diversity of lived experience adds truth and innovation to the dialogue. Be sure to actively think about and include those whose opinions and backgrounds are different than yours. Because we don't need more choirs who only sing one kind of music, do we?

Start with a beginner's mind. Walk into the conversation with a sense of curiosity about others at the table. (Remember, everyone has a 7-minute story.) Agree not to try to change each other's minds, but instead practice deep listening to inform how you participate in the dialogue.

Be open to the experience of others and suspend judgment. Yes, this can be tough. Depending on the topic and power dynamics in the room, this can be incredibly challenging. It's so much easier to cancel, unfriend, or hide behind tweets. It's so much riskier to stay in the dialogue. Cancel culture is everywhere and the ultimate expression is walking away from the table and shutting voices out. There are all kinds of legitimate and real reasons for this, many rooted in self-preservation. Stay in it anyway.

Your mindfulness practice comes in handy here. As your blood starts to boil and a reactionary response percolates, a mindful leader will automatically sense this, understand it for what it is, and take the opportunity to pause and instead choose a thoughtful response. This takes practice and is an invaluable skill to hone.

This powerful James Baldwin quote comes to mind: "We can disagree and still love each other, unless your disagreement is rooted in my oppression and denial of my humanity and right to exist." As a white woman, I'm the first to recognize that the choice to stay is easier for me to make. I have learned to deeply understand that for people of color, the fight is always and everywhere and exhausting. In the suggestion to "stay in it," I want to offer grace and discernment depending on your circumstances. Only you can know and trust that knowing.

Consider this question when you are in the heat of courageous conversations: If you walk away now, could you be leaving five minutes before the miracle happens? Imagine the ROI if we could push through to the other side of our discomfort, letting tough love, empathy, courage, and compassion teach us.

The ALF Way Applied

In 2017, ALF hosted a nearly 300-person community dialogue on gun safety. We intentionally invited folks on all sides of the issue, from gun club enthusiasts to participants in the March for Our Lives movement who advocate aggressively for gun violence prevention. Our staff trained dozens of volunteer facilitators in ALF-style dialogue, with instructions on table group agreements and guidelines for the conversations.

About forty tables of six to eight participants, with varying life experiences and political views, came together purely to seek to understand vs. change each other's minds. "Experts" were discouraged from oversharing; everyone was given a turn to speak.

One attendee who was a self-proclaimed second amendment advocate and gun enthusiast decided to chance it and attend, as there were "so few spaces to have dialogue and really hear each other," he later told me. While he had a heart for what March for our Lives stood for, he would never dare walk up to a protestor at a live rally and try to engage in a conversation.

He sat at a table next to a teacher, who in recent years had to guide her young students through active shooter drills. She came with very firm and opposing views about the National Rifle Association. Because the table was set with alternative viewpoints, and because the facilitators created a brave space to hold productive tension, in order to truly hear and stay in it, a number of things happened.

Perspectives shifted because those who had judged or canceled second amendment advocates heard new narratives and began to understand the frustration of "gotcha" gun policies and poorly designed regulation. Those who dismissed the arguments of "left-leaning do-gooders" began to hear painful stories and frustrations about the lack of common-sense regulation that resulted in bloodshed and trauma for young people in particular.

A critical policy recommendation came from this community day of mindful dialogue: a 24/7 safe surrender program in Santa Clara County that would offer a way for suicidal individuals and their loved ones, in particular, to get rid of guns quickly. 80% of gunshot wounds in the county were self-inflicted, and there did not exist an easy way to surrender firearms. With this policy shift anyone, for any reason, could turn in a gun safely and for any reason, without reprisal.

And who thought up the smart gun policy recommendation? The self-proclaimed second amendment advocate and gun enthusiast. So yeah, mindful dialogue can work.

We are facing the intersection of extraordinary crises as a global community, from climate change to the rise of authoritarianism to a deadly pandemic that is debilitating our economy. We have a choice of how we show up to problem-solving circles and who gets a seat at those tables. If we can pivot from exclusionary, monolithic board rooms to empathetic and curious dialogue spaces rooted in mindfulness and active listening, we have the opportunity to transform outcomes for communities and even countries, for generations.

CONCLUSION

By **ADAM TORRES**

Business leaders come from many backgrounds. Their stories are infinitely varied. Along the way, they experience success and failure. Some of the leaders presented are further along their leadership path than others, but one common trait is shared among all of them. They are never done working on their craft. They continue to push forward to test the boundaries of what they think they are capable of. Above all, this one trait will be responsible for much of the innovation that occurs in our generation and the generations that follow. Leadership is fundamental to our future success, not only in business but in our society at large.

To your success,

Adam Torres

P.S. If you'd like to apply to be a guest on one of our shows visit **MissionMatters.com/PodcastGuest** to apply.

APPENDIX

Adam Torres | Foreword | Page iii
Co-Founder Mission Matters
MissionMatters.com
Instagram: @AskAdamTorres
Twitter: @AskAdamTorres

Christine Churchill Burke | Chapter 1 | Page 1
Founder and CEO of the Customer Service Institute of America
christine.churchill@ServiceInstitute.com
LinkedIn (Company): Customer-Service-Institute-of-America
LinkedIn (Personal): christine-churchill-burke
Instagram: CustomerSrvInstofAmerica
Facebook: @serviceinstituteofamerica
website: serviceinstitute.com
Financial Cost of Bad Service Whitepaper: https://www.serviceinstitute.com/the-financial-cost-of-bad-service/

Dan Fusco | Chapter 2 | Page 11
Founder, InnerPC
MYinnerPC.com
Dan@myinnerpc.com
https://www.linkedin.com/in/innerpc/
https://www.facebook.com/innerpc/

David Andras | Chapter 3 | Page 19
World Gym Northeast Ohio (Akron, Brooklyn, Sheffield Village)
dave.andras@worldgym.com
Facebook: @worldgymsheffield, @worldgymbrooklyn, @worldgymakron
Twitter: @worldgymfit
Instagram: @worldgymsheffield, @worldgymbrooklyn, @worldgymakron
www.worldgym.com
Northern Ohio Business Center
david@nobc.info
Facebook: @NorthernOhioBusinessCenter
Twitter: @center_northern
Instagram: @northernohiobusinesscenter
www.nobc.info

Founder and Chief Visionary at A Bolder Vision:
www.aboldervision.com
jen@aboldervision.com
Twitter: @aboldervision
Facebook: https://www.facebook.com/aboldervision
Instagram: aboldervision

José Manuel "J.M." de Jesús | Chapter 8 | Page 67
President and CEO
Quadrant Two PR LLC
PRManJM@gmail.com
Twitter: @QuadrantTwoPR, @PRManJM
LinkedIn: http://www.LinkedIn.com/in/jmdejesusmba

Kimberley J. Daly | Chapter 9 | Page 77
Franchise Consultant
kim@thedalycoach.com
Website: thedalycoach.com
LinkedIn: www.linkedin.com/in/dalykim
Facebook: www.facebook.com/createwealththrufranchising
YouTube: KimDaly.tv

Patricia Baronowski-Schneider | Chapter 10 | Page 87
President/CEO, Pristine Advisers
http://www.pristineadvisers.com/
YouTube: https://www.youtube.com/user/PristineAdvisers/videos
Vimeo: https://www.youtube.com/user/PristineAdvisers/videos
LinkedIn: https://www.linkedin.com/company/1674911 & https://www.linkedin.com/in/patriciabaronowski/
Facebook: https://www.facebook.com/PristineAdvisers?sk=wal
Twitter: https://twitter.com/pristineadvise1
Instagram: https://www.instagram.com/pristine_advisers/
Blogs: https://pristineadvisers.medium.com/

Roman Tsarovsky | Introduction | Chapter 14 | Page vii, 127
Founder and CEO of Ally Inc.
Email: roman@allynow.com
Website: https://Allynow.com
Facebook: https://www.facebook.com/orderally
Twitter: https://twitter.com/orderally
Instagram: https://www.instagram.com/allyplatform/
LinkedIn: https://www.linkedin.com/company/allyinc
Telegram: https://t.me/AllyNow

Russell G. Luce | Chapter 15 | Page 137
Founder, Planning Legacies Financial Group
Russell@PLFG.org
Twitter: @RLUCE721
LinkedIn: linkedin.com/in/Russellgluce/
Facebook: facebook.com/Russellluce

Sharif Almamun | Chapter 16 | Page 143
Twitter: @almamun_sharif (https://twitter.com/almamun_sharif)
FB: https://www.facebook.com/sharif.almamun.161
LinkedIn: https//www.linkedin.com/in/sharifalmamun
President and CEO, iLynx
Website: https://www.ilynxinc.com
Twitter: @iLynxInc (https://twitter.com/ilynxinc)
LinkedIn: https://www.linkedin.com/company/ilynxinc
Founder, Impact with Sharif Almamun video podcast series
YouTube: www.youtube.com/channel/UCSsb9Bmy302SbqAQyyjJYXA

Suzanne E. Kecmer | Chapter 17 | Page 153
Founder & CEO SKB Capital
Suzanne_Kecmer@skbcapital.com
Website: skbcapital.com
LinkedIn: https://www.linkedin.com/in/skecmer/
Twitter: @SKBCapital

Suzanne St. John-Crane | **Chapter 18** | Page 165
CEO of American Leadership Forum Silicon Valley
Board Chair of ALF National
suzanne@alfsv.org
Twitter: @alfsv, @stjohncrane
Facebook: alfsiliconvalley
Instagram: @alfsiliconvalley
Linkedin: alfsv, suzannestjohncrane
The Dialogue podcast: alfsv.org/podcast/
Youtube: alfsiliconvalley

Listen to our
PODCASTS

MISSION MATTERS
WE AMPLIFY STORIES

www.MissionMatters.com

OTHER AVAILABLE TITLES

In this latest edition of *Mission Matters (Women in Business Edition Volume 1)*, Torres features 18 top female professionals who share their lessons on business and leadership. In these pages, through inspiring stories, you'll discover:

- Why empathy and EQ is crucial in leadership
- How failure paves the way to success
- How to find your purpose
- How to turn your passion into your life's purpose
- What it means to turn challenges into gifts
- What value-based care means for cancer patients
- And much more!

Purchase at **MissionMatters.com**.

In the forth edition of *Money Matters (Business Leaders Edition Vol 4),* Adam Torres features 18 top professionals who share their lessons on leadership. In these pages, through inspiring stories, you'll discover:

- How patient care and technology meet in the medical field.
- How digital transformation is imperative for companies.
- What creating your dream retirement looks like.
- How to create a result-driven culture in your company.
- How to pivot your marketing to survive crisis situations.
- Why cohesion is more important than engagement in an organization.
- And much more!

Purchase at **MissionMatters.com.**

In the third edition of *Money Matters (Business Leaders Edition Vol 3),* Adam Torres features 13 top professionals who share their lessons on leadership. In these pages, through inspiring stories, you'll discover:

- Different approaches to leadership and people management.
- Rules for success from a Green Beret.
- How to effectively manage a company full of millennial employees.
- How to transform your marketing mindset.
- Where customer success and employee success meet.
- What manifesting your success in business looks like.
- And much more.

Purchase at **MissionMatters.com.**

In the second edition of *Money Matters (Business Leaders Edition Vol 2)*, Adam Torres features 18 top professionals who share their lessons on leadership. In these pages, through inspiring stories, you'll discover:

- How to harness the entrepreneurial mindset.
- Why scaling your business for sustainable growth is vital.
- How to grow your eCommerce business.
- Lessons learned from sales experts.
- How to level up your leadership.
- How to manage your energy.
- And much more.

Purchase at **MissionMatters.com**.

Navigating the world of real estate can be stressful. Are you getting closer or further away from your goals?

Adam Torres is here to help you move forward. In his latest edition of *Money Matters (Real Estate Edition Volume 2)*, Torres features 13 top professionals who share their lessons in real estate.

In these pages, through inspiring stories, you'll discover:
- How to get more properties through syndication.
- How to implement servant leadership to have a more successful business.
- Why investing in real estate is not just for rich people.
- How important insurance is in real estate transactions and what to look for.
- Why using a private lender can help you in real estate transactions.
- What legal options you have to protect your assets.
- And much more!

Purchase at **MissionMatters.com**.

In the original edition of *Money Matters (Business Leaders Edition)*, Adam Torres features 15 top professionals who share their lessons on leadership. In these pages, through inspiring stories, you'll discover:

- How to create a clear path for growth.
- Why every business should act like a media company.
- How to build a community to last a lifetime.
- Lessons learned from professional soccer.
- How to maintain a well-connected brain for peak performance.
- How to create harmony through union in business.
- And much more.

Embracing diversity and inclusion in a rapidly changing business landscape can be challenging. Are you and your organization positioned properly for this new age of connectivity? Torres features fourteen top Asian leaders who share their lessons on diversity, equality and inclusion.

Navigating the world of real estate can be stressful. Are you getting closer or further from your goals? Finance guru Adam Torres is here to help you move forward. His guide, Money Matters, features 15 top professionals who share lessons from their more than 250 years of combined experience.

In this clear, concise manual, financial expert Adam Torres goes over the basics of personal finance and investing and shows you how to grow your wealth. Torres makes sure you are prepared for whatever life throws your way. It's never too early to think about the future and his book will give you the right tools to tackle it.

All books available for purchase at **MissionMatters.com**.

This workbook has been designed specifically for individuals like you who are dedicated to improving the results in all areas of your life. By following the ideas and exercises presented to you in this transformational workbook, you can move yourself into the realm of top achievers worldwide.

Download for free at **MissionMatters.com**